Engaging Activities

to Teach Phonics

and Phonological

Awareness

Includes additional literacy skills and activities!

by

Deborah Diffily and Charlotte Sassman

Carson-Dellosa Publishing, Inc.

Greensboro, NC

Credits

Editor:
Kelly Gunzenhauser

Layout Design:
Van Harris

Inside Illustrations:
Marty Bucella
Bill Neville

Cover Design:
Annette Hollister-Papp

ISBN 1-59441-377-0

Table of Contents

Introduction 4

Awareness of Sounds and Words 9

Letter Recognition 17

Rhyming Words 33

Consonant/Sound Correspondence 51

Vowel/Sound Correspondence 86

Initial and Final Sounds of Words 126

Onset and Rime 150

Blending... 168

Segmenting 178

Sight Words... 191

© Carson-Dellosa • CD-104165

Introduction

Learning to read is perhaps the most important task of elementary-age students. Early childhood educators recognize their responsibility to teach necessary literacy-related skills so that students progress into competent readers. This book does not address ways to support young children's language development. Rather, it starts at the next step as children begin paying attention to the parts of spoken language. This book also acknowledges these important facts:

- there are many different tasks that must be accomplished in order to learn to read;
- students learn these tasks in different orders;
- students have different learning styles;
- teaching reading is best accomplished by using activities to suit a variety of learners.

PRE-READING SKILLS

Within the task of learning to read are dozens of complex, interrelated skills. Although these skills are not directly hierarchical, there are typical patterns. As soon as children begin to talk, adults support their oral language development and model standard English by describing what children are doing, extending their one- or two-word comments into more complex statements, and by asking open-ended questions. For example, when a toddler points to a ball and says, "Ball," the adult often says something like, "That's right, point to the ball," "Do you want me to give you the ball?" or "Would you like to play with the ball?" Note also that the words in children's spoken vocabularies are the words that they learn to read more easily.

Typically in preschool, when provided with appropriate learning experiences, students begin learning to pay attention to parts of spoken language. Learning the sounds of spoken language is directly related to students' later ability to decode written words. The understanding that oral language can be divided into smaller components and manipulated is called *phonological awareness*. This important concept is one that young children must master on their way to becoming competent readers.

Phonological awareness can be grouped into four primary categories, and students tend to master them in this order: dividing sentences into words (sentence segmentation), dividing words into syllables, identifying individual phonemes, and manipulating phonemes. Manipulating the sounds of language also includes deleting, adding, or substituting syllables or sounds. Having phonological awareness means that students possess an understanding of all of these levels of dividing spoken language. While students do not always learn different tasks of phonological awareness in the same way, the next section describes typical phonological awareness learning.

The skills at the less complex end of the phonological awareness continuum are rhyming words and sentence segmentation. After that, the tasks include dividing words into syllables and blending syllables into words. Next is the ability to segment words into onsets and rimes and blending onsets and rimes into words. At the most complex end of the phonological awareness continuum is phonemic awareness. Phonemic awareness involves the understanding that words are made up of individual sounds (phonemes), as well as the ability to manipulate the sounds of words by segmenting, blending, or substituting individual sounds within words to create new words. The National Research Council's report on reading differentiates phonological awareness from phonemic awareness by stating: "The term *phonological awareness* refers to a general appreciation of the sounds of speech as distinct from their meaning. When that insight includes an understanding that words can be divided into a sequence of phonemes, this finer-grained sensitivity is termed *phonemic awareness*" (Snow, Burns, & Griffin, 1998, p. 51).

Students demonstrate their development of phonological awareness in several ways, by:
- Identifying and making oral rhymes:
  "The cat is wearing a (hat)."
  "The man in the (van)"
  "Fun in the (sun)"
- Identifying and working with syllables in spoken words:
  "I can clap the parts in my name: Jor-dan."
- Identifying and working with onsets and rimes in spoken syllables or one-syllable words:
  "The first part of fun is f."
  "The last part of wing is -ing."
- Identifying and working with individual phonemes in spoken words:
  "The first sound in bat is /b/."

ORGANIZATION OF THIS BOOK
The literacy-related activities in this book are loosely organized by skill in the same order that students generally learn them. Beginning with the simplest area (Awareness of Sounds and Words), it continues to the most complex (Sight Words). Between these two sections are Letter Recognition, Rhyming Words, Consonant/Sound Correspondence, Vowel/Sound Correspondence, Initial and Final Sounds of Words, Onset and Rime, Blending, and Segmenting. Under each section, a variety of activities include: whole group activities, small group activities, games, songs and rhymes (including finger plays), active learning experiences, manipulatives, file folder activities, and transitions.

Teachers constantly look for a variety of teaching strategies, realizing that their students have different ability levels and learning styles. Some students learn best through songs and rhymes, others through playing games. Some students learn best when information is presented orally, and others need to manipulate objects in order to remain focused on the task at hand. *Engaging Activities to Teach Phonics and Phonological Awareness* addresses these various learning styles and offers multiple ways to teach literacy.

EXPLANATION OF ACTIVITY TYPES

Whole-group learning experiences can be quite varied and range from very simple to very complex. Perhaps one of the simplest learning experiences is helping students pay attention to a specific sound, not necessarily the sounds associated with letters, but familiar environmental sounds. Other whole-group learning experiences include read-alouds of picture books, poems, songs, or chants, with a special focus on phonological awareness, phonemic awareness, or phonics. Specific lessons for the entire class typically introduce concepts or offer practice with skills that most of the students in the class need to practice. However, since most of the time literacy-related lessons are best taught in small groups, it is also appropriate to teach whole-group activities to small groups. (See below.)

As stated above, phonological awareness and phonics lessons are best taught to **small groups** because the learning experiences can be more closely targeted to meet students' specific needs. These targeted lessons are effective with small groups, peer partners, or as homework suggestions for families. Most of the activities are also appropriate for a volunteer or tutor who is working with one student or a small group.

Kinesthetic learners learn best with **manipulative objects** that they can touch or move, that are related to the concept being taught. These activities offer different ways to manipulate actual letters and objects that represent letter sounds. Letter tiles, buttons, dice, dominoes, interlocking cubes, and index cards are used to support students as they learn to manipulate the letter sounds they hear. These manipulative activities are best presented to small groups since they help students focus and also eliminate the need for a large number of manipulatives.

Playing games is a particularly effective way to motivate students to practice skills. Most students need repeated experiences with the association of letters to sounds before consistently remembering them. Rather than requiring monotonous skill drills, games provide a method of practice that students enjoy. Games can be offered during self-selected center time, assigned to small, homogenous groups, or sent home as family homework.

File folder activities can be made available as a choice for students in a language learning center or assigned to individual students who need further practice with certain letters/letter sounds. Extra copies of these activities can be created and sent home for additional practice.

Songs and rhyming chants offer special opportunities for students' language development. Students are drawn to music and tend to learn lyrics fairly easily. Use songs to teach particular concepts, or enjoy them just for the rhyme or rhythm they provide.

Most of the activities listed above call for the students to actively participate. However, those that are hands-on, require movement, and do not specifically use game boards or manipulatives are labeled as **active learning**. When students are actively involved, they learn skills and concepts more easily and remember them for longer periods of time.

There are always times when teachers find themselves with a few extra minutes to "fill" until a specific designated time. For example, classes cannot show up for lunch five minutes early; teachers who teach "specials" or mini-classes are not always ready at the moment a class arrives outside their doors; an in-class lesson may take less time than the teacher planned for, etc. These **transition** ideas can be used for times like this, or to help make smooth transitions between activities within the classroom.

There are also **teacher tips** scattered throughout the book. These will give hints on how to find materials, organize or execute some of the activities, and improve the impact of lessons.

 **Teacher's Helpers**, offset by the owl and an oval shadow, include literature selections, word lists, and short resource lists for activities.

Most activities in this book can be set up in learning centers so that students who need additional experience with a particular skill can work on this skill independently or with a partner. When students are engaged in learning experiences that are at their individual ability levels, the teacher has the opportunity to differentiate instruction by working with individuals and small groups of students. Note that some activities fit into more than one category. For example, some of the file folder activities are also games, some of the songs involve movement, etc. For simplicity's sake, each activity is categorized by the most relevant learning style it addresses.

CHOOSING APPROPRIATE LEARNING EXPERIENCES FOR STUDENTS

Not all students need to be involved in every learning experience mentioned in this book. Too many early childhood educators teach literacy-related skills to entire classes. While some whole-group instruction is acceptable, the majority of literacy-related skills should be taught to students within their zone of proximal development: the area between what students know and can do independently and what students can do with the support of an adult or more competent peer. Teaching within a student's zone of proximal development is most effective.

Teachers who direct their teaching to each student's zone of proximal development must routinely assess each student's skills and note the areas where the student has confusion or needs additional support. This assessment can be done formally with instruments such as a primary reading inventory, or informally noted as a teacher confers individually with a student about his reading. Most teachers use a combination of approaches and keep some type of anecdotal record about each student's skills. When inconsistencies are noted, the teacher can turn to the appropriate section of this book for suggestions about teaching the needed skill. This helps the teacher target her instruction directly to the student's needs and provides a quick reference for teaching daily reading skills. (For more information about informal assessments, refer to page 147.)

While every student does not learn literacy skills in the exact same order, the following list represents the order in which students commonly learn these skills. This list can help determine which particular skills should be taught and at what time.

1. Recognizes letters by name.
2. Recognizes a few letters by sound (/b/ for the letter *b*, for example).
3. Recognizes rhyming sounds and alliteration in simple words.
4. Identifies when the first letter sound of a word is different from the first letter sound of another word.
5. Blends simple word parts together to form a word. Student also distinguishes a lowercase letter from an uppercase letter.
6. Blends individual letter sounds together to form a word.
7. Segments, or separates, a word sound by sound.
8. Understands how changing letters in a word changes the sounds and the meaning.
9. Sounds out one-syllable words with short and long vowel spellings.
10. Sounds out multisyllabic words.

When a student demonstrates any one of these skills, it is time to begin providing learning experiences related to the next skill in this list.

At the end of each section is an assessment form that can be used to document each student's learning. It is important to monitor students' progress on a regular basis in order to make instructional decisions that are best for each student. For example, a teacher should not begin teaching onsets and rimes until a student can identify rhyming words, or begin teaching segmenting sounds in words until a student can identify initial sounds in words.

Awareness of Sounds and Words

Many reading experts now believe that when very young students have certain literacy-related learning experiences, they create circuits in their brains that support the process of learning to read. Sally Shawitz (2003, p. 67) wrote, "reading relies on brain circuits already in place for language." These circuits are created through appropriate experiences related to oral language. Listening and speaking are the beginning experiences students need as the foundation for literacy development.

Students begin establishing brain circuits for later reading development when they learn to listen and repeat what they hear. Most students begin this development as infants or toddlers. As infants, some children mimic cooing sounds made by their primary caregivers. Even more children (as toddlers) learn to repeat common words when prompted. These are the children who come from homes where children are valued and adults place a high priority on interacting with them. However, some children do not have this type of home environment. These children, especially, benefit from a rich oral language environment in preschool and primary classes. Regardless of the source, students need to be surrounded by language. They need adults who talk with them, listen to them, and purposefully extend their language by modeling complex, standard English sentences. Additionally children need adults who introduce new vocabulary through concrete experiences. This is because students'

literacy development is built on this basis of learning the sounds of language. The following activities will help students practice their listening skills and participate in oral language experiences. The assessment (page 16) will help you determine students' skills in these areas. Use the assessment before or after using the activities.

Hearing and Naming Sounds

Use a small, handheld recorder to record a variety of environmental sounds from outdoors, from the classroom, and from your home. Some examples of possible sounds are listed below. Ask students to close their eyes as you play one sound at a time. Encourage students to identify each sound.

- a ball bouncing on the gymnasium floor
- a meowing or purring cat
- an alarm clock ticking, then ringing
- a barking dog
- feet walking down the hall
- frying bacon
- a cooing pigeon
- a whistling teakettle
- boiling water
- rustling leaves

Extension – Assign students to small groups. Provide pictures of the things making the sounds. (Cut them from magazines or use an instant or digital camera to photograph them.) Have students select the correct picture that matches each sound, instead of naming what made the sound.

Extension – Place the audiotape, a set of headphones, and the pictures in a listening center and ask students to complete this activity independently or in pairs.

Same-Sound Jars

Collect plastic film canisters or small, opaque, plastic containers with lids. Fill two canisters with the same object(s), such as a jingle bell, an acorn, four paper clips, 10 kernels of popcorn, three dried lima beans, the same amount of sand, the same amount of rock salt, the same amount of salt, etc. Identify matching sound jars by marking a small dot on the bottom of each canister in a set with the same color of paint pen or nail polish. Place the canisters in a center. During a quiet time, have students take turns shaking the sound jars and matching the pairs that sound the same. When they finish sorting the sound jars into pairs, show them how to look on the bottoms of the jars for the matching, colorful dots to confirm that they sorted the canisters correctly by sound.

Clapping Patterns

When learning to pay attention to sounds, students benefit from hearing and repeating rhythmic patterns by clapping their hands, slapping their knees, or snapping their fingers. Use this transition activity as an attention-getter for large-group instruction. Have students sit in a circle with their legs crossed. Ask them to pay close attention to what you do, then demonstrate a pattern, such as clap-clap-slap-slap. Then, ask students to join you in repeating the pattern.

Search for Sounds

Take students on a walking field trip to search for sounds. Take a chart paper tablet and a marker, and walk with students around the school's neighborhood, or just around the playground if your school does not allow walking field trips. Tell students to listen carefully. After five or six minutes outside, have students brainstorm a list of sounds they hear. Have students recreate those sounds as you write them down.

Extension – If possible, brainstorm a list of possible sounds students might hear on their next field trip, and then ask students to listen for the sounds they listed. Check off each sound as students identify it. If a field trip is not possible, try asking students what sounds they would expect to hear in different places: at the zoo, in the woods, in a city, or on a farm. Have them make those sounds as you list them.

Composing

Play different selections of songs that have strong rhythms. Encourage them to pretend to be instruments by making their own sounds, such as taps, clucks, or claps, along with the songs. Marches and other songs with loud drumbeats or bass lines work well for this activity.

Teaching Tip

In addition to teaching students to listen to and repeat sounds, use the Clapping Patterns activity to teach different patterns, such as ABABAB, ABBABBABB, ABCABCABC, etc. Students can use letter manipulatives to make the patterns, then say the pattern rhythmically while looking at the manipulatives.

Fishing for Words

Use this activity to introduce important classroom objects. As you hold a butterfly net, lead students around the classroom to "fish" for words. Place the net around a new object in a learning center, such as a bucket, and say (or sing), "I've caught a bucket, a bucket, a bucket." Have students repeat after you as you take the object out of the net and place it on a nearby table. Repeat this for at least three more items. As students practice listening and repeating words, they also learn new vocabulary words to help them describe their interactions with concrete materials in the classroom. If you focus on theme-related materials and do this activity on the first day of each new theme, students will benefit from learning new words related to each theme.

Extension – After you have led this activity several times and students learn the routine, give the butterfly net to one of the students and let him "catch" a few items.

Packing for a Trip

Place a collection of items related to a current classroom theme in the middle of a small group. Model this activity by holding a small suitcase (or duffle bag, briefcase, or backpack) and saying, "I'm going on a trip and I am packing _____ for my trip." As you say this sentence, pick up one of the items, name it in the sentence, then place it in the suitcase. Pass the suitcase to the student sitting on your right. He should repeat your sentence, then select an item and say the sentence again. Keep passing the suitcase, repeating sentences, and adding sentences as long as students can remember the preceding sentences.

Extension – As students learn the alphabet, reinforce it with a similar version of this game. Post a copy of the alphabet near the group. Let students take turns packing imaginary items using alphabetical order. One student should say, "I am going on a trip, and I am taking an alligator," or other object beginning with the letter A. The next student should say, "I am going on a trip and I am taking an alligator and a baseball bat," or other object beginning with the letter B. Continue through the letter Z, with the last player repeating the entire list. Students should be encouraged to help each other remember sentences.

Teaching Tip

This activity is based on memory as much as it is based on learning to name new objects. Initially, this game should be played with two or three students, so that students only need to remember a few sentences. Increase the number of students in the small group and/or the number of objects over time.

Matching Sounds to Objects

Create audiotapes of about 10 sounds that are familiar to most students, such as a car starting, a person whistling, a can of soda being opened, popcorn popping, etc. Cut out pictures from catalogs or magazines of the things that make each of those sounds, and glue each picture to a separate index card. Laminate the cards for durability. Challenge students to sequence the cards in the order that they hear the sounds.

Ordering the Bells

Gather 15 small jingle bells and five envelopes. (You can also use padded envelopes or small, opaque containers, such as plastic butter tubs.) Put one bell in the first envelope, two in the second envelope, etc. Seal the envelopes. Write the number of bells in each envelope on the sticky side of a self-stick note, and attach it to the envelope. Place the envelopes in a learning center. Challenge students to organize the envelopes by sound in order from softest to loudest. Have them look at the backs of the self-stick notes to check their work.

Guess Who?

This activity helps students focus on listening skills. Tape-record several different students talking, singing, or reading, one at a time. Have each student say something different so that you can easily identify the speaker. Play the tape of each student speaking several times and allow students to guess which classmate they hear.

Extension – To make this a live-action activity, select one student to be "it." Blindfold the student and have her classmates stand around her in a circle. Point to one student in the group and have him say a predetermined sentence in his regular voice. Allow the student who is "it" to guess the name of the speaker. If she is correct, consider letting her try to explain why she knew who was speaking.

Name That Tune

Ask students to be very quiet. Point to one student and ask her to hum one line of a familiar song. Encourage her classmates to raise their hands as they recognize the song. Let the student who hummed part of the song choose a classmate to guess the name of the song. If that classmate correctly names the song, it becomes her turn to hum. If she does not correctly name the song, the student should hum the first and second lines of the song and choose another classmate to guess.

13

Hints

Use this activity to reinforce positional words and prepositions. Hide an object in the classroom. Give very specific hints about where to find the object. Allow the first student to find the object to choose the next hiding place.

Musical Bottles

Fill four identical glass bottles with different amounts of water. Put the bottles and a rhythm stick or mallet in a learning center. Allow students to tap the bottles with the stick, then order the bottles according to the sounds they hear, from lowest pitch to highest pitch. When students can do this, add additional bottles of water to make the task more challenging.

Sound Words

Read aloud a book that uses onomatopoeia: words that describe sounds made by animals, vehicles, or objects. Just as you encourage students to join in "reading" repeated lines in books, encourage students to chorally read these sound words when they appear in the book. Suggestions for this type of book are in the Teacher's Helper section: Books with Sound Words.

Teacher's Helper: Books with Sound Words

Baby-O by Nancy White Carlstrom (Little, Brown, 1994).
In this rhymed, cumulative text, Carlstrom tells about a West Indian family gathering produce to take to the market. Sound words in the text create a delightful read-aloud for young students.

City Sounds by Craig Brown (Greenwillow, 1992)
A farmer's day in the city offers a symphony of sounds from tugboat horns and train whistles to sirens and jackhammers, and finally the "peep peep peep" of small baby chicks.

City Sounds by Rebecca Emberley (Little, Brown, 1989)
Emberley presents onomatopoetic rhythms from a day in an urban neighborhood. A toaster goes pop and high heels go tip-a-tap. The book also has a glossary of sounds.

Cock-A-Doodle-Doo! What Does It Sound Like to You? by Marc Robinson (Stewart, Tabori, & Chang, 1993).
Common sounds such as a dog's bark, a train whistle, and dripping water are presented in several different languages, such as English, Spanish, Chinese, and Hebrew.

Down by the Cool of the Pool by Tony Mitton (Orchard Books, 2002)
Frog, Duck, Horse, and Pig spend their time dancing, flipping and flopping, splishing and splashing, and wiggling and waggling down by the cool of the pool.

Hush! A Thai Lullaby by Minfong Ho (Scholastic, 2000)
In this story of a mother trying to keep things quiet so that her infant continues to sleep, noisy animals continue to peep, squeak, cry, and shriek. Each animal has its own unique sound.

Mice Squeak, We Speak by Arnold Shapiro (Putnam, 1997)
Every page of this book shows an animal making its own particular noise, such as, "Flies hum. Dogs growl. Bats screech. Coyotes howl. Frogs croak. Parrots squawk. Bees buzz." In the end, people speak.

Off We Go! by Jane Yolen (Little, Brown, 2000)
One by one, baby animals leave their homes and head to their grandmothers' houses. The noisy text mixes sound and movement as snakes slither-slee, moles dig-deep, and so on.

Polar Bear, Polar Bear, What Do You Hear? by Bill Martin, Jr. (Henry Holt & Co., 1991)
Zoo animals are asked what they hear. Each answer is a sound word, such as a fluting flamingo and a hissing boa constrictor. The zookeeper also "hears" students dressed as their favorite animals.

Assessment of Awareness of Sounds
Children develop awareness of skills at different times. As students work on the activities listed above in teacher-led small groups or centers, use the form (page 16) to document observing a student who uses each of these five skills: identifying environmental sounds, matching sounds, hearing and repeating clapping patterns, hearing and repeating vocabulary words, and hearing and repeating sound words.

Assessment of Awareness of Sounds

Student's Name	Identifies Environmental Sounds	Matches Sounds	Hears and Repeats Clapping Patterns	Hears and Repeats Vocabulary Words	Hears and Repeats Sound Words

Letter Recognition

Whether a student can correctly name the letters of the alphabet is one of the best predictors of a student's early reading success. Young students need multiple opportunities to manipulate and explore three-dimensional letters. Magnetic letters on large cookie sheets, blocks imprinted with letters, letter-shaped sponges (to paint letter collages), and alphabet puzzles are all excellent learning materials for students to use to explore and experiment with concrete portrayals of letters. However, students also need to hear adults talk about the letters they are using, so that, over time, students begin associating a specific name for each letter.

Initially, young students tend to learn the letters that are most important to them. Usually a student will learn to recognize the first letter of his first name before any other letter. Neuman, Copple, and Bredekamp (2000) state that "long before they go to school, young children can learn to spot letters important to them, such as the 'S' in Sesame Street or the 'Z' of zoo" (p. 65). Young students may also learn "D" for Dad or "M" for Mom because these words are important to them. Other letters that students initially learn depend on the experiences that are provided for them, the people they know, and the environmental print they see.

The learning experiences listed below can be offered to preschoolers, but there should not be the same expectation for remembering the letters that teachers have for kindergartners and first-grade students.

Letters to Play With

Children learn from play, so provide many opportunities for them to play with letters. Early childhood educators should make different types of letters available, such as letter blocks, beanbag letters, sponge letters, lacing bead letters, magnetic letters, etc., for students to manipulate and explore. Students can build with alphabet blocks in the block center, toss beanbag letters into containers or at targets labeled with corresponding letters, use letter sponges to stamp paint onto individual papers or on large pieces of paper to create a group mural, string alphabet beads onto necklaces, or stick magnetic letters on cookie sheets, filing cabinets, or a magnetic board. Also stock this center with letters to trace, alphabet stamps, alphabet puzzles and games, picture cards, alphabet books, flash cards, erasable boards, alphabet cassettes and a few cassette players, clay, paints, and any other materials that support learning about letters. As students play, be sure to comment on letter names to help students learn them.

"Feely" Letters

Use a die-cutting machine to cut out letters from various materials, such as felt, sandpaper, sponge, foil, burlap, etc. Then, place the letters in a center. The differences in appearance and texture will encourage students to handle them.

Sorting Letters

Students who have had few experiences with the alphabet need extra support in "playing" with letters. Help students pay attention to the details of how letters are constructed. First, create sorting mats. Label a sheet of construction paper "Letters with Only Straight Lines." Label a different color of construction paper "Letters with Some Curved Lines." (Be sure to explain the difference between curved and straight, if necessary.) Place the papers and a set of uppercase letter manipulatives on the floor in the middle of a small group. Ask each student to find one letter that has only straight lines (A, E, F, H, I, K, L, M, N, T, V, W, X, Y, Z) and put that letter on the appropriate sorting mat. Help each student name the letter he places on the mat. Encourage students to keep looking for letters with straight lines, by saying things such as, "I see three more letters with only straight lines. Look carefully, and I think you can find them." After all of these letters have been placed on the sorting mat, challenge students to find the letters that have some curved lines (B, C, D, G, J, O, P, Q, R, S, U) and place those on the appropriate sorting mat. Continue naming the letters as students place them on the sorting mat. As students get more proficient, create a third mat labeled "Letters with Only Curved Lines." Help students identify the letters that fit this category (C, O, S). (The letters U and J have curves at the ends of their straight lines, so students may encourage you to create a fourth category for these letters.)

> **Teaching Tip**
>
> As you name the letters for students in Sorting Letters, extend your comments by pointing out classmates' names that begin with those letters. For example, say, "This letter is J. Jonathan and Julia's names start with the letter J."

Making Letters

In a learning center, place chenille craft sticks, Wikki® Sticks, play dough, clay, or lengths of yarn dipped in white glue and placed on sheets of waxed paper. (Students can shape the glue-coated yarn into letters on the waxed paper and leave them to dry.) Display an alphabet poster, a set of alphabet cards, or the Alphabet Recognition Chart (page 19) in the center. (If students are using anything sticky, do not let them handle the cards or poster without first washing and drying their hands.) Encourage students to make alphabets of their own from the different materials.

Alphabet Recognition Chart

A B C D E F G H I

J K L M N O P Q R

S T U V W X Y Z

a b c d e f g h i

j k l m n o p q r

s t u v w x y z

● ● What's in a Name?

The letters of their first names are typically the most important letters to young students. Provide plenty of experiences for students to work with the letters in their names. Write a student's name on a piece of card stock, naming each letter as you write it. Also, provide different art supplies for students to decorate their own name tags. Post name tags on students' cubbies, on artwork, beside class jobs, on center assignment charts, or on an attendance chart. Create name crowns by writing each student's name on a sentence strip and stapling the strip together to fit the student's head. Whenever possible, point to the letters of a student's name and encourage the student to repeat after you.

Extension – Let students form groups according to the first letters of their names. Then, choose a student from each group to name letters under which other students are grouped.

B-I-N-G-O

Copy the traditional song "Bingo" on chart paper (see below). Teach the song by pointing to the words and letters as the class sings along. Make multiple letter cards for *B, I, N, G,* and *O* on 4" x 6" index cards. After students learn the song, give each student one of the letter cards. Sing the song slowly a couple of times to give students time to react by holding up their letters as they are sung. (Students should not raise their letters when they are replaced in the song with claps.) Over time, students will learn to recognize these letters.

There was a farmer had a dog
And Bingo was his name-o.
B-I-N-G-O, B-I-N-G-O, B-I-N-G-O,
And Bingo was his name-o.

There was a farmer had a dog
And Bingo was his name-o.
(clap)-I-N-G-O, (clap)-I-N-G-O, (clap)-I-N-G-O,
And Bingo was his name-o.

Leave out an additional letter during each of the following four verses.

Beat Me to the Top of the Coconut Tree

After reading *Chicka Chicka Boom Boom* by Bill Martin, Jr. (Simon & Schuster Books for Young Readers, 1989), remind students that all of the letters ran up to the top of the coconut tree. Provide brown and green paper for each student to create her own coconut tree on a separate piece of paper. Provide magazines or catalogs and scissors for each small group. Ask students to find the letters in their names, cut them out, and glue them so that they appear to "climb" their trees. As students work, focus on helping them connect the sounds to the letters in their names.

Extension – Provide a set of large uppercase and lowercase letter stencils. Let each student select a letter in both uppercase and lowercase from the set, trace the letters on construction paper, and cut them out. Then, let her draw a coconut tree on a separate piece of paper. Glue the letters so that they appear to climb the tree. Collect the papers and bind them to create a class ABC book.

Matching Uppercase and Lowercase Letters

Write uppercase and lowercase letters on round counters, such as plastic lids from gallon milk cartons or soda bottles. Let students match appropriate uppercase and lowercase letters.

Extension – When beginning this activity, it may be difficult for students to distinguish between uppercase and lowercase letters. Writing the letters on two-sided counters normally used in math activities can help. Simply write all of the lowercase letters on the red side and the uppercase letters on the yellow side.

Beautiful Alphabet

Add to your class set of alphabet books and introduce students to books written and illustrated by Jan Brett at the same time. Go to the alphabet section of her Web site (http://www.janbrett.com/alphabet/alphabet_main.htm) and print out her illustrations of objects for each letter of the alphabet. Use a color printer, if possible, although these will also reproduce nicely in black and white. Post them on a bulletin board or collate them to create another alphabet book to add to the class collection.

> **Teaching Tip**
> The counters you create for the Matching Uppercase and Lowercase Letters activity can be used to assess students' letter recognition knowledge instead of the printed assessment at the end of this section (page 31).

Homemade "Magic" Writing Board

Use resealable, plastic bags to create fun, colorful, "magic board" writing surfaces that students can use over and over. To make one magic board, reinforce the three sealed edges of the plastic bag with colorful masking tape. Put a small amount of finger paint inside of the bag. (Mix the paint colors in each bag to add variety. Add a bit of liquid starch if the paint is too thick.) Close the bag and reinforce that edge with tape, as well. Let students "write" on the bag by squeezing the paint as they drag their fingers across the bag to form letters. Smooth the bag's surface to easily erase the letters. Use these in a variety of ways. Begin by saying a letter and asking students to "write" it. Or, display a picture of an object, say its initial, final, or medial sound, and instruct students to write the corresponding letter. Students can also direct their own activity by writing a letter and challenging each other to provide a word that begins (or ends) with that sound.

Seven in a Row

Form a small group and provide the group with a set of alphabet letter tiles. Ask each student to draw seven letters and place them in a column on the left-hand side of the playing area. Then, draw a letter tile, show it to the students and pronounce its name. Have each student repeat the name and, if she makes a match, move the matching tile to the right side of her playing area. Play continues until a student is able to move all of her letters to the right side.

ABC Motion

While students are jumping rope, using the seesaw, swinging, marching around the room, or using the stairs, lead them in reciting the alphabet. Keeping the beat helps students say each letter clearly and helps prompt them from one letter to the next.

Teaching Tip

Enlist help in making the "magic" writing boards. Ask a parent volunteer to put the masking tape on three sides and to spoon a bit of paint into each bag. Then, let students seal the bags, add tape to the closed edge, and smooth out the bags.

Teaching Tip

In the Seven in a Row activity, if working with seven letters is confusing, begin play by selecting only three or four letters. Increase the number of letters as students' skills improve.

Alphabet Mats

Use this activity to assess students' knowledge of the alphabet. To make an alphabet mat, trace the outline of small plastic letters, in order, across the top of a long piece of paper. On the rest of the paper, draw a large arch that is long enough to hold all of the letters of the alphabet. Give each student a mat and the set of plastic letters. At first, ask them to match the letter with its outline. Notice and assess which students can name the letters and which ones just match the shapes. Also, notice which students know which letters come at the beginning or end of the alphabet and which ones come in the middle. As the students become familiar with this activity, ask them to put the letters in order on the arch.

Highlighting Letters

Print a letter (both uppercase and lowercase) on an index card. Ask a student to name the letter. If he cannot, name the letter and ask the student to repeat it. Have him look for the letter in newspapers or magazines and mark each occurrence with a highlighter. Repeat with different letters for other students in the group. After a few minutes, ask students to "read" their letters to each other.

Name Chants

Students' names are very important words to them, and they learn to use personal chants quickly. Use the traditional chant, "A, my name is Alice," (below) as a model for creating chants for each student in the class. Use these personal chants to dismiss students from the group area to centers or to call them to group meetings.

A, my name is <u>Alice</u>, (Insert student's name.)
And my <u>husband's</u> name is <u>Arthur</u>, (Insert the appropriate spouse and name.)
We come from <u>Alabama</u>, (Insert place name that begins with appropriate letter.)
Where we sell <u>artichokes</u>. (Insert letter-appropriate item.)

Teaching Tip

Before giving students a page from a newspaper or a magazine for Highlighting Letters, skim the pages and make sure there are several examples of those letters on the page. Also, be sure to use sections of the materials, such as advertisements, that have large print for easy highlighting.

Letter Search with Environmental Print Cards

Gather a wide selection of environmental print (coupons, advertisements, front panels from food boxes, can labels, junk mail, menus, etc.), and a set of 4" x 6" index cards. Mount one example of environmental print (names of common products and stores that students will recognize) on each index card. Laminate the cards for durability. Gather students near an alphabet chart. Model choosing one letter from the alphabet, then searching through the environmental print cards for a sample of that letter. (Students will recognize the initial letters first.) Have every student in the group look at the letter and repeat its name after you.

Extension – Confirm that every letter of the alphabet is represented in the cards you created. After students are familiar with this activity, challenge pairs or small groups to locate one environmental print card for each letter of the alphabet, in order.

The Alphabet Song, Part II

Write each uppercase and lowercase letter in large black print on the upper-left side of a large piece of paper. Over several days, ask students to draw the objects listed below. When all are finished, post these drawings on the wall where every student can see them. Then, teach them this song sung to the tune of "The Alphabet Song." Point to each letter as it is sung.

> ### Teaching Tip
>
> Send a few examples of environmental print cards home to each student's family. Encourage them to make more cards so that their child can practice identifying and naming letters of the alphabet. If families do not have access to supplies needed to make the cards, send home packets of index cards, scissors, a glue stick, and magazines or food labels and containers.

"The Alphabet Song, Part II"

a, a, apple	m, m, man
b, b, ball	n, n, nickel
c, c, cat and	o, o, ox and
d, d, doll	p, p, pickle
e, e, egg and	q, q, queen and
f, f, fan	r, r, rail
g, g, goat and	s, s, sun and
h, h, hand	t, t, tail
i, i, inchworm	u, u, umbrella
j, j, jam	v, v, vase
k, k, king and	w, w, wagon in a race
l, l, lamb	x, x, x-ray and
	y, y, yard
	z, z, zoo
	now, that wasn't so hard!

ABC Relay

Assign students to two teams. Write the letters in alphabetical order on two sentence strips and post each strip on the board or other magnetic surface. Provide a container of magnetic letters at the front of the room for each team. Signal for the first student on each team to walk to the front of the room, select a letter, place it over the corresponding letter on the alphabet strip, and return to her team, tagging the next person to repeat the process. Play continues until all of the letters have been placed. The last student must verify the sequence of the letters. The first team to successfully place all of the letters wins.

> **Teaching Tip**
> Laminate the alphabet strips used in ABC Relay and use them for several additional activities (below).

Extension – To make the game harder, have students place the letters in a row without the help of an alphabet strip.

Closer to Z

Provide an alphabet strip (see ABC Relay, above) and a full set of letters (magnetic, foam, plastic, or paper cutouts) for each pair of students. Instruct both students in each pair to put half of the letters in their laps. Explain that the letter selection should be random. Tell each pair to place the alphabet strip faceup so both students can see it. To begin the game, let each player place a letter on the desk at the same time and say the name of the letter. Players should refer to the alphabet strip if needed, then the player with the letter closest to the letter *z* should say, "_____ is after _____ and closer to *z*. I win." The winner then collects both of the letters and places them in a separate pile. The game continues until all of the letters are gone. The winner of the game is the student with the most letters.

Extension – The pairs can also play Closer to A so that the letter closer to *a* is the winner or Closer to M so that the letter closer to *m* is the winner. If students' letters are equal distances from *m*, it is a tie and they each get to keep their own letters.

Line Them Up

Pair students and provide each pair with an alphabet strip (see ABC Relay, above) and two containers of letters. Place the *m* and *n* in the center of the playing surface. Then, let each student draw five letters, without looking, and take a turn placing her letters before or after the *mn* pair. Each time a student places a letter, he should say, "_____ comes before (or after) _____." Play continues with students drawing letters from the "pile" and rearranging them as necessary to keep them in alphabetical order. The first student to run out of letters is the winner.

Touch and Say

Provide each group with a small, opaque container of plastic letters. Have a student close his eyes and pick a letter from the container. Ask him to feel the letter without looking at it, then try to name the letter correctly. If he names the letter correctly, he should keep the letter. If his answer is incorrect, he should return the letter to the container, and the next student should take a turn.

What's Missing?

On a magnetic board, ask a small group of students to arrange a set of magnetic letters in alphabetical order. While the students cover their eyes, remove a letter. Then, call on a student to identify and replace the missing letter by writing it in the blank. If the task is too challenging, introduce the activity using smaller groups of letters. For example, arrange the *h, i, j, k, l, m, n, o,* and *p* magnets on the magnetic surface. Grouping the letters to coordinate with the traditional ABC song offers students additional support as they learn this letter identification skill. Have students sing the song to find out what is missing.

Extension – A metal baking sheet makes a good surface for magnetic letters. Buy several that are the same size and stack them inside each other to store them. Many stores that sell merchandise for a dollar sell magnetic letters. If magnetic letters and a board are not available, the game can also be played with letter cards on the chalk tray or in a pocket chart.

Teaching Tip

To simplify the Touch and Say activity, place only the letters students are studying in the container. Limiting the choices of letters reinforces the skills currently being taught. Add more letters to the container as additional letters are introduced. Also, when introducing the activity, place the letter into the student's hand so that each letter is right-side-up and facing in the correct direction.

Go Fishing for Letters

Use index cards to make a "Go Fish" deck of 104 letter cards, with four of each letter in the deck. (All letters can be uppercase or lowercase, or can be a mix if students can recognize them.) Shuffle the deck and deal six cards to each player. (Use fewer cards if students have trouble holding them, or cut index cards in half to make smaller playing cards.) The first player can ask any other player for one letter that he has in his hand. If the second player has the card, she must give it to the first player and the first player gets another turn. If the second player does not have the card, she says, "Go fish," and the first player must take one card from the top of the deck. Play continues until one player gets four of the same letter.

Extension – Have players use letter sounds instead of letter names when they ask each other for cards.

Alphabet Bingo

Use the Alphabet Bingo Grid (page 28) to create bingo playing cards. Let each student fill in the grid by writing a different letter in each space, in any order. Use pennies or other counters for game pieces. Play Alphabet Bingo with three or four students. Call out one letter at a time, writing it as it is called so that there are no repeats. The student who covers all of the letters on the game card and calls out, "Bingo," wins the game.

Extension – Call out letter sounds instead of letter names.

Where Has the Letter Gone?

Put three or four alphabet cards in strange places in the classroom, such as on a window sill or taped to the clock face. Sing the following lyrics to the tune of "Oh Where, Oh Where Has My Little Dog Gone?"

Oh, where, oh, where has our letter "A" gone?
Oh, where, oh, where can it be?
It is on a card that we had all along,
Please find it and show it to me.

Just before starting a new verse, assign a student to find the alphabet card for the letter being sung about. Or, for students who are more familiar with the letters, instruct students to walk around the classroom to locate letters in any order. As they find them, let students raise their hands and sing the song.

Hangman

Hangman is a popular game for students, but is often overlooked for students just learning to name letters of the alphabet. Use words that have some meaning for the class, such as word wall words or short words associated with a current unit of study. Draw an underlined space on the board for every letter in the selected word. Tell students to look at the number of letters in the word and to refer to the word wall for ideas. Allow students to take turns guessing one letter at a time until all spaces are filled in. List letters that are guessed, but are not in the word, on the board also. As you do this, say the letter names for students who have not yet learned to name the entire alphabet.

Extension – You can also draw the traditional stick figure to make the activity into more of a game. Draw one body part for each missed letter, and write each missed letter next to its corresponding body part.

> ### Teaching Tip
>
> After creating teacher-made games such as Go Fish or Bingo, laminate game boards and pieces for durability. When cutting out the materials after laminating them, leave $1/16$" (1.6 mm) of laminate extending beyond the paper edges to prevent the laminate from separating.

Alphabet Bingo Grid

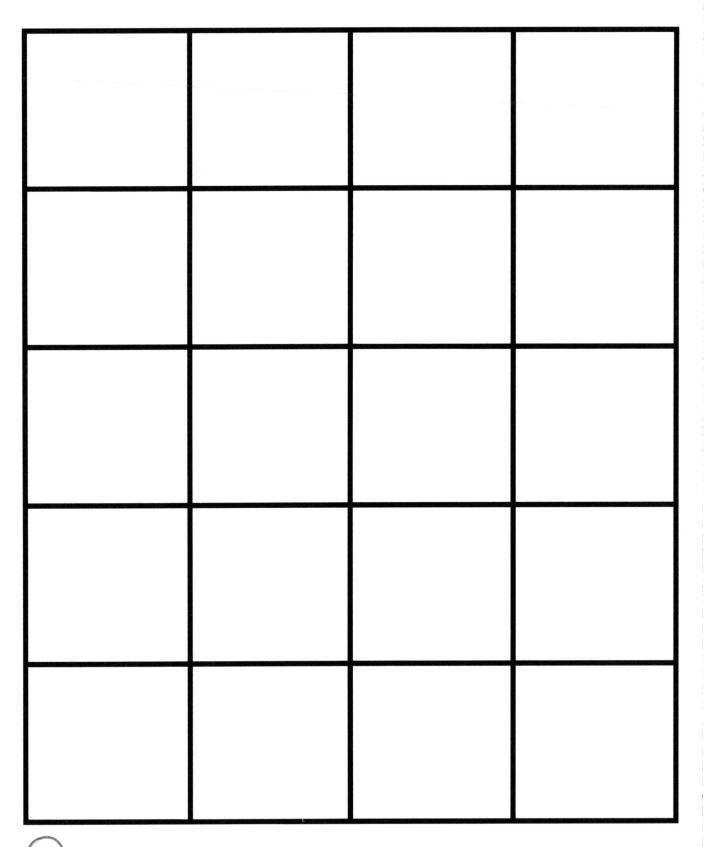

Picking up an "A"

Singing helps students remember letter identification. When introducing a letter name, make enough copies of that letter for each student to "pick up" and "put back down" as they sing this song to the tune of "The Paw Paw Patch."

Picking up an "A" and putting it in the basket,
Picking up an "A" and putting it in the basket,
Picking up an "A" and putting it in the basket,
Way down yonder in the letter patch.

Extension – When most students have learned letter names, extend this activity by adding a second verse and singing the letter sound instead of the name.

Picking up an /a/ and putting it in the basket,
Picking up an /a/ and putting it in the basket,
Picking up an /a/ and putting it in the basket,
Way down yonder in the letter patch.

Finger Spelling Alphabet

To keep the interest of students who can name all letters of the alphabet while other students are catching up, check out the book, *The Handmade Alphabet* by Laura Rankin (Dial Books, 1991), or enlarge copies of the Finger Spelling Alphabet reproducible (page 30). Challenge those students to learn the finger spelling sign for each letter of the alphabet, then have students learn to spell their names.

Teaching Tip

Make letter manipulatives for Picking Up an "A" by writing letters on index cards. For students who are more visual learners, it is better to create letter shapes, perhaps using die-cut letters and laminating them for durability. To prevent confusion resulting from reversals, cut letters from two different colors of construction paper and laminate the two letters together. Then, instruct students to "turn the letters to the red side" so that the letter cards face the correct way.

Finger Spelling Alphabet

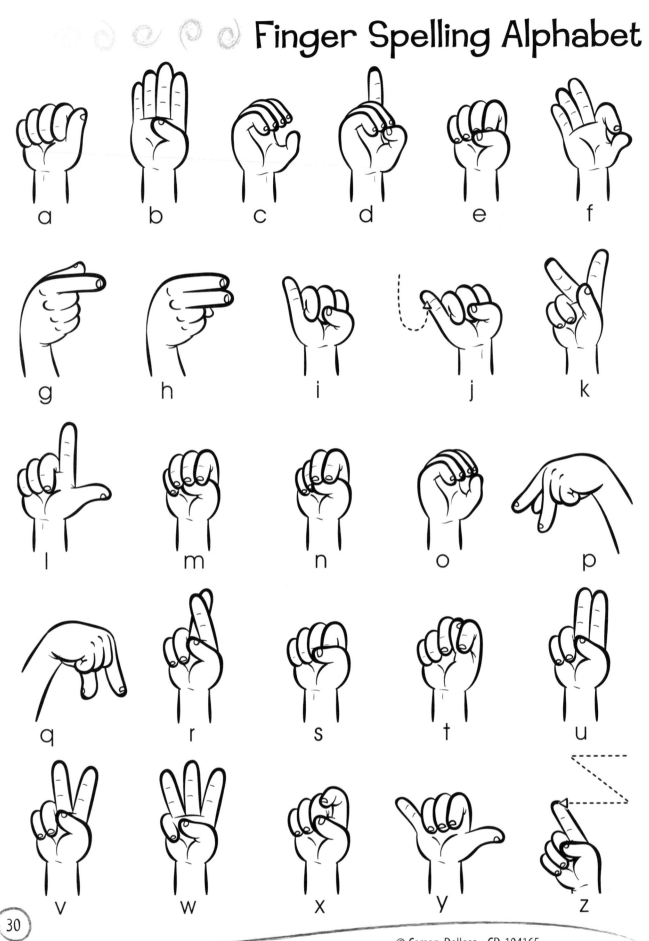

Assessment of Letter Recognition

Name _____   Date of Birth _____

Recorder _____   Date _____

Show the student the letters on the following page, one row at a time. If the student correctly names the letter, put a check mark in the LN (Letter Name) column. If the student correctly says that letter sound, put a check mark in the S (Sound) column. If the student can name a word that starts with that letter, write that word in the W (Word) column. If the student gives an incorrect answer, record what the student said in the IR (Incorrect Response) column. Students can be assessed on one, two, or all three concepts at any given time.

Uppercase Letter	Letter Name LN	Sound S	Word	Incorrect Response IR	Lowercase Letter	Letter Name LN	Sound S	Word	Incorrect Response IR
A					a				
F					f				
K					k				
P					p				
U					u				
Z					z				
B					b				
G					g				
L					l				
Q					q				
V					v				
C					c				
H					h				
M					m				
R					r				
W					w				
D					d				
I					i				
N					n				
S					s				
X					x				
E					e				
J					j				
O					o				
T					t				
Y					y				

A	F	K	P	U	Z
B	G	L	Q	V	
C	H	M	R	W	
D	I	N	S	X	
E	J	O	T	Y	

a	f	k	p	u	z
b	g	l	q	v	
c	h	m	r	w	
d	i	n	s	x	
e	j	o	t	y	

Rhyming Words

The ability to recognize rhyming words is part of *phonological awareness*. Phonological awareness—the awareness of speech sounds—is directly related to reading success (Opitz, 2000). Some toddlers develop the ability to recognize and even create rhyming words. These students typically grow up in language-rich homes, where nursery rhymes and other poems are an integral part of adult/child interaction. Students who do not have these experiences at home need multiple opportunities at school to interact with rhyming words in songs, chants, nursery rhymes, and other poems, and assorted informal language activities described in this section.

Music is often used to help students learn and then practice rhyming words. Musical activities can be used to help students learn academic content, especially in literacy development (Smith, 2000). Many children's songs contain rhyming words that can be highlighted as the songs are learned. These songs can then be used as models to help students rewrite rhyming lines.

Students can typically identify two rhyming words before they can produce a rhyming word from a one-word prompt. Students usually acquire this second skill after multiple experiences of hearing several rhyming words in the same pattern. After a student is able to identify rhyming words from a couplet, model brainstorming additional words to match the couplet's rhyming pattern. The following activities will give students practice in hearing, identifying, and finally in creating rhymes.

Couplet Rhymes

Select rhymes that use couplets, such as the traditional song "This Old Man," to make the rhymes more obvious to students.

This old man, he played one,
He played knick-knack on my thumb.

Chorus:
With a knick-knack paddywhack,
Give a dog a bone.
This old man came rolling home.

Additional Verses

Two, shoe	Seven, 'til eleven
Three, knee	Eight, gate
Four, door	Nine, spine
Five, hive	Ten, once again
Six, sticks	

Extension – Write this poem on chart paper as a rebus (using numerals and sketches in place of the objects in the verses) so that students can "read" the chant.

Extension – On a set of index cards, write the numbers 1–10. Tape a picture of each object from the song to an index card to create a picture card set. Put the cards in a learning center and encourage students to put the rhyming pairs together.

Whispering Poems

After ensuring that all students know particular nursery rhymes or poems, start the day by reciting one or two. Emphasize the rhyming words by whispering all of the words except for those that rhyme. Say those words loudly. Or, chant in a normal voice, then whisper the rhyming words.

Extension – Write these familiar rhymes and poems on chart paper and point to words as students recite them. Knowing that they are "reading" the words correctly boosts emergent readers' confidence in their reading abilities.

Extension – Type rhymes and poems on 8.5" x 11" paper, making enough copies for each student in the class, plus a few extras. Distribute copies to students and ask them to "read" the poems. Put a copy of each poem in a three-ring binder labeled "Our Class Poetry Book." Send copies of the poem home and encourage parents and students to keep Poetry Folders and read a few poems from them several times each week.

Teaching Tip

If students do not know nursery rhymes or other children's poems, take a few minutes each day to teach one to the class and review one or two from previous days. Most young students remember simple rhymes after a few repetitions over several days. There are also many children's books that contain adaptations of nursery rhymes. Gather these books together in a basket labeled "Rhymes and Poems." Encourage students to "read" these books independently.

Rhyming Concentration

Copy the Rhyming Concentration cards (pages 35-36) on card stock. Cut out each square. Laminate the cards for durability. Let students take turns turning over two cards at a time, and looking for two rhyming pictures. If a student finds a match, he should keep the cards and take another turn. (Note that each pair of matching cards has a unique symbol in the lower right-hand corner to make the activity self-checking.) If his pair does not match, he should replace the cards. It is then another player's turn. Play concentration with students in small groups, then put the Rhyming Concentration cards in a learning center and encourage students to play this game on their own. Picture names are *knee, three, dog, log, bat, cat, can, fan, cake, rake, egg, leg, moon, spoon, crib, bib, mug, bug, five, hive, tree, bee, goat, boat*. If desired, review the picture names with students ahead of time.

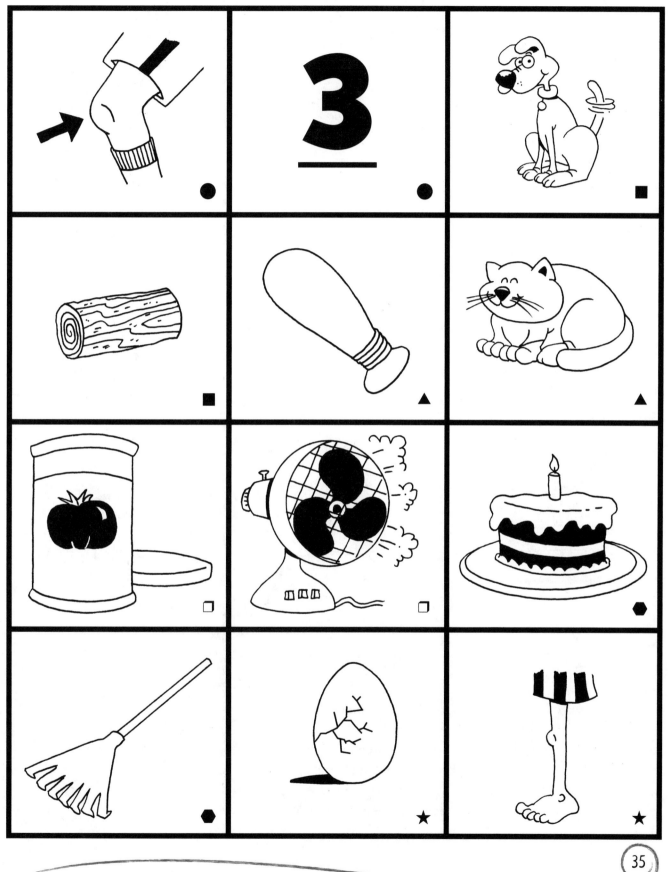

Rhyming Pairs

After reading a book to students, choose words from the story and play Rhyming Pairs. For example, if the book is *The Very Hungry Caterpillar* by Eric Carle (Philomel Books, 1994), say these word pairs:

egg - leg   egg - ball

cheese - please   moon - dark

leaf - tree   leaf - beef

If the pair rhymes, students should stand up. If the pair does not rhyme, students should sit down.

Extension – After students have had many experiences hearing and identifying rhyming words, say a word and ask students to say words that rhyme.

Extension – When students become more proficient at supplying their own rhyming words, let a student supply the original word, and allow classmates to come up with rhymes. Consider choosing one student a day to think of a word for other students to rhyme. Write the original word on the board and list students' rhymes underneath. Leave all of the rhyming words posted to create a rhyming word wall.

Word Detectives

After students begin to demonstrate that they can hear and identify rhyming words, choose a book with many rhyming pairs, such as *The Cat in the Hat* by Dr. Seuss (Random House, 1957). Read the book to a small group of students. Ask them to close their eyes and listen carefully for the words that rhyme. After you read once for content, reread the book and help students list the rhyming words they hear on each page.

Class-Made Rhyming Book

Students love to be the originators of rhymes, so give them the opportunity to make a rhyming book of their own. After students have sufficient experience learning and reciting rhyming poems, playing rhyming games, and hearing adults read quality picture books that feature rhyming text, lead them to brainstorm pairs of rhyming words. Let each student choose one rhyming pair, and write each pair at the top of a piece of paper. Ask students to illustrate their words. Create a front and back cover for the book, bind it, and place it in the class library for students to read independently.

> **Teaching Tip**
>
> Even after students become skilled at hearing rhymes, they do not always provide real words when asked to produce a rhyme. Often, a student will offer a nonsense word, such as *jat* to rhyme with *bat*. This is okay. The most important thing is hearing and producing rhymes, not recognizing the real words they invent.

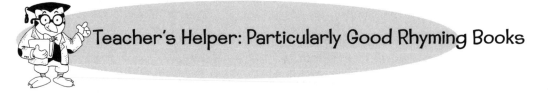

Teacher's Helper: Particularly Good Rhyming Books

Reading entertaining rhyming books that capture students' attention can help them develop rhyme awareness. The following books are entertaining and contain many rhyming words.

The Cat Barked? by Lydia Monks (Puffin, 2001)
A cat bemoans his life until his owner points out that the cat would be unhappy as anything else.

Counting Crocodiles by Judy Sierra (Gulliver Books, 1997)
This retelling of the traditional tale describes a monkey who outwits a crocodile.

Chicken Soup With Rice: A Book of Months by Maurice Sendak (HarperTrophy, 1991)
Sendak combines simple rhymes and a repeated verse to create a poem for every month. This book is also available on audiocassette.

Cows in the Kitchen by June Crebbin (Candlewick Press, 1998)
While the farmer sleeps, animals invade the farmhouse. The repetitive text, animal sounds, and rhythm and rhyme will engage young students.

Drummer Hoff by Barbara Emberley (Simon & Schuster, 1967)
In this Caldecott Medal winning tale, as soldiers join Drummer Hoff, they bring objects that rhyme with their names.

Farm Flu by Teresa Bateman (Albert Whitman & Company, 2001)
This humorous rhyming story tells of a young boy left alone to take care of the farm. When the animals come down with the flu, he cares for them with bed rest and tummy rubs.

"I Can't," Said the Ant by Polly Cameron (Scholastic, 1961)
An ant's ingenuity helps get a fallen teapot repaired and back safely on the countertop. Items in the cupboard utter rhyming words of encouragement.

Is Your Mama a Llama? by Deborah Guarino (Scholastic, 1997)
Steven Kellogg's drawings preview answers to Guarino's rhyming riddles about mother and baby animals.

The Lady with the Alligator Purse by Nadine Bernard Westcott (Little, Brown, 1990)
In this version of the jump-rope rhyme, Tiny Tim swallows bath water. The doctor prescribes penicillin and the nurse suggests castor oil, but the lady with the alligator purse thinks pizza will solve the problem.

Math for All Seasons by Greg Tang (Scholastic, 2002)
Every poem is also a math question. The rhyming questions help students group and count objects.

Miss Mary Mack by Mary Ann Hoberman (Megan Tingley, 1998)
Hoberman's adaptation of the traditional chant includes several new verses.

Moving Day by Robert Kalan (Greenwillow, 1996)
In short, rhythmic rhymes, Kalan tells the story of a hermit crab looking for the perfect home.

The M & M®'s Brand Counting Book by Barbara Barbieri McGrath (Charlesbridge, 2002)
This rhyming book uses familiar candy to teach numbers 1–12, six colors, and three basic shapes.

Mice Squeak, We Speak by Arnold Shapiro (Putnam, 1997)
Tomie dePaola's paintings illustrate Shapiro's brief rhyming text based on what animals "say."

Off We Go! by Jane Yolen (Little, Brown, 2000)
Several baby animals journey to Grandma's house. Each animal's rime creates a clear rhyming pattern.

One fish two fish red fish blue fish by Dr. Seuss (Random House, 1960)
This childhood favorite follows a loose story line and emphasizes many rimes. Examples of the same rime are grouped on one or two pages, so teachers can focus their lessons on one particular rime at a time.

Pigs in the Mud in the Middle of the Rud by Lynn Plourde (Scholastic, 1997)
A family tries to get their Model T Ford around the pigs in the mud. Finally, Grandma is successful.

Pumpkin Eye by Denise Fleming (Henry Holt & Co., 2001)
Fleming's text is driven by rhyme, rhythm, and eerie Halloween imagery.

The Shark Who Was Afraid of Everything by Brian James (Scholastic, 2002)
This rhyming story describes Sharkie, who meets Lily the Little Fish. She helps him to be brave.

Splish, Splash, Spring by Jan Carr (Holiday House, 2002)
Collages and rhyming text depict students' spring activities: watching birds, digging up worms, picking flowers, flying kites, and playing in the rain.

Three Little Kittens by Lorianne Siomades (Boyds Mills Press, 2000)
Illustrations similar to finger paintings depict this classic Mother Goose rhyme.

Daily Poetry Read-Alouds

Designate a particular time every day as Poetry Time. Poetry Time could be a transition between content area lessons, or between lunch or recess and the next lesson. At the beginning of the year, focus on poetry with a strong sense of rhyme and rhythm. Use the books below and also any of your own favorites.

Particularly Good Poetry Books That Feature Rhyme and Rhythm

Bing Bang Boing: Poems and Drawings by Douglas Florian (Puffin, 1996)
Florian wrote and illustrated 150 poems on topics range from bugs to monsters. Many of these poems for grades 4-6 include word play appropriate for younger students.

The Llama Who Had No Pajama: 100 Favorite Poems by Mary Ann Hoberman (Browndeer Press, 1998)
Hoberman's poems range from very short to very long in this silly and amusing collection.

Laugh-eteria: Poems and Drawings by Douglas Florian (Puffin, 2000)
Florian offers young readers another collection of amusing poems. His creative word usage occasionally includes made-up words that continue the rhymes.

Surprises by Lee Bennett Hopkins (HarperCollins, 1986)
Hopkins contributes poetry and also serves as the editor for this collection of short poems by Marchette Chute, Myra Cohn Livingston, Aileen Fisher, and others. This was designated a 1984 Notable Children's Book by the American Library Association.

Take-Home Books

Create a take-home lesson to provide some at-home rhyme time. Provide multiple copies of particularly good rhyming books and poetry books for students to check out and take home. Encourage families to read these books to their students.

Dr. Seuss Week

Celebrate Mr. Geisel who was so very "wisel." Read two Dr. Seuss books each day for a week. Select a few lines from each book and repeat those until students remember them. Focus on rhyming couplets and be sure to include a few of Seuss's invented words.

Teaching Tip

Before sending books home with students, be sure to teach them how to care for books. Sending books home in gallon-sized, heavy, resealable, plastic bags or in pocket folders helps protect them from damage.

Mary had a little lamb,
Its fleece was white as sn___.
And everywhere that Mary went,
the lamb was sure to g—.

Reading "Cloze" Rhyming Words

Write a familiar nursery rhyme or poem on chart paper. For the rhyming words, write the initial letter, blend, or digraph, and a blank underline for the rest of the word. As the class reads the poem aloud, have students say the word that they think belongs in each blank.

Extension – Instead of the rhyming words, write one key word in each line as a "cloze" word. Point to each word as students recite the rhyme. Point out that they are reading those words by using the initial letter sounds and their memories. Key words could include word wall words or words that are particularly difficult for students to read independently.

Word Family Rings

Give students some word family practice. Using the Word Family Ring Cards (page 43), enlarge and cut out the cards from one word family, laminate them, punch a hole in each, and connect them with a small metal ring. Make six sets of each word family for small groups to use for practice in reading the word family words. Assign one student in each group to read the words as the others repeat them. Word families on the reproducible include -ad (b, f, h, l, m, p, s), -an (b, c, f, m, p, r, t, v), -at (b, c, f, h, m, p, r, s, v), -it (b, f, h, k, l, p, s, w), and -in (b, f, k, p, t, w). Trace the cards and cut out blank ones to create other word family sets.

Did You Ever See?

Sing the following lyrics to the tune of "If You're Happy and You Know It."

Did you ever see a (cat) in a (hat)?
Did you ever see a (cat) in a (hat)?
No, I never, no, I never, no, I never, no, I never,
No, I never saw a (cat) in a (hat).

Did you ever see a (duck) in a (truck)?
Did you ever see a (duck) in a (truck)?
No, I never, no, I never, no, I never, no, I never,
No, I never saw a (duck) in a (truck).

Repeat with ring/swing and rake/cake. After singing these verses, challenge students to come up with their own rhyming pairs to create new verses.

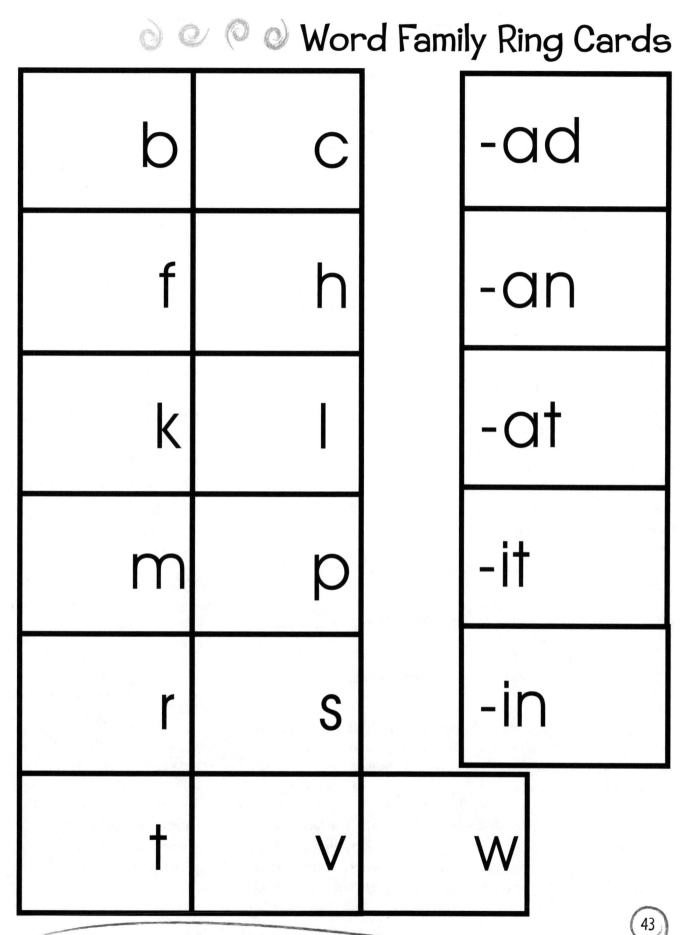

b	c
f	h
k	l
m	p
r	s
t	v

w

-ad

-an

-at

-it

-in

One of These Things Is Not Like the Others

Working in groups of three or four students, show four picture cards where three of the pictures' names rhyme and one does not. Then, explain that one of these things is not like the others. Ask a student to point to the card that is different and say why it does not belong with the other three. For example, a student might say, "The picture names of bat, cat, and hat all rhyme, but dog does not rhyme with them."

Extension – This game can be played with picture cards related to language concepts other than rhyming words. Consider playing this game with initial, medial, or ending sounds of words, beginning blends, or digraphs.

Down by the Bay

Many singers, songwriters, and writers have written and performed different versions of the traditional song "Down by the Bay." Teach students the lyrics below as an example, then ask the class to help you make up more of your own.

Down by the bay, where the watermelons grow,
Back to my home, I dare not go.
For if I do, my mother will say,
"Did you ever see a goose kissing a moose,
down by the bay?"

Down by the bay, where the watermelons grow,
Back to my home, I dare not go.
For if I do, my mother will say,
"Did you ever see a whale with a polka-dotted tail,
down by the bay?"

(Other possible verses include *fly wearing a tie, bear combing his hair, llamas wearing their pajamas,* and *Did you ever have a time when you couldn't make a rhyme?*)

Extension – For songs like "Down by the Bay," write the lyrics on chart paper and challenge students to search for certain characteristics among the lyrics, such as repeating words, words that rhyme, or words in a certain category (in "Down by the Bay," that category could be animal names). Focus on one characteristic at a time and have students highlight the words that they find.

Five Monkeys at the Zoo

There are several different verses and versions of "Five Little Monkeys." Teach students a different version, or use the one below to teach words that end with the long /e/ sound.

Five little monkeys, sitting in a tree,
Teasing Mr. Alligator, "You can't catch me!"
Along came Mr. Alligator, quiet as can be.
He SNAPPED that monkey right out of that tree.

Repeat with four, three, and two monkeys, then for the last little monkey, say, "'Yum,' said Mr. Alligator, 'I'm as full as I can be!'"

Extension – Using hand motions will help students remember this rhyme more easily. Support your arm by holding up the "tree;" that is, use one hand to support the other forearm and hand with five fingers waving to be the "teasing monkeys." Then, as the alligator comes, use both hands to make a snapping alligator's mouth.

Getting Ready to Go Home Chant

When it is time to pack up at the end of the day, many early childhood educators lead the chant:

Clean up, clean up
Everybody, everywhere,
Clean up, clean up,
Everybody do their share.

To reinforce the concept of rhyming words, teach students the following extension of the chant. Use it as students are packing up their belongings at the end of the school day or as they prepare to leave the room. Add your own rhymes as needed to tailor the chant to your classroom.

Pick up the blocks, blocks, blocks
Don't watch the clocks, clocks, clocks.
Put all of the books, books, books
Back in their nooks, nooks, nooks.
Put on your jacket, jacket, jacket
Don't make a racket, racket, racket.
Walk down the hall, hall, hall
And that is all, all, all.

Traditional "Hickory, Dickory, Dock"

Make rhyming more rhythmic with sound effects. Sing or chant the nursery rhyme below with students. Use a ticking clock, rhythm sticks, or even a non-digital metronome to simulate the sound of a ticking clock. Add a bell or small gong to make the sound of the clock striking one.

Hickory, dickory, dock.
The mouse ran up the clock.
The clock struck one,
The mouse ran down.
Hickory, dickory, dock.

Extension – Emphasize the -ock rime, or use words that emphasize the -an, -ick, or -uck rimes.
Extension – Help students hear that *one* and *down* do not rhyme. Brainstorm a list of words that rhyme with one and down. Emphasize that the meaning would change if either of these words were replaced.
Extension – Change the lines, "The clock struck one, the mouse ran down," to make them rhyming couplets, such as "The clock struck two, the mouse found a shoe," or "The clock struck three, the mouse was free." Encourage students to make up their own lines.

"A-Hunting We Will Go"

Teach students to sing "A-Hunting We Will Go" to the tune of "The Farmer in the Dell."

Oh, a-hunting we will go,
A-hunting we will go,
We'll catch a fox
And put it in a box
And then we'll let it go.

Have students identify two words that sound the same (*fox/box*). Sing the song with other pairs of rhyming words, such as *whale/pail*, *frog/log*, and *fish/dish*. Pause at the second rhyming word and let students sing the rhyme. To continue the lesson, ask students to brainstorm other animals for the song. List the animals on chart paper, then brainstorm a rhyming object for each one. Examples could be: *snake/lake/cake/rake* or *bear/hair/dare/chair*. Use the list to model creating new lines for the song. For example: "We'll catch a snake and put it in a lake," or "We'll catch a bear and hug it if we dare." Next, write the following verse on chart paper or an overhead transparency:

Oh, a-hunting we will go, a-hunting we will go.
We'll catch a _____ and put it in a _____ ,
And then we'll let it go.

Help pairs of students use copies of the "A-Hunting We Will Go" reproducible (page 47) to create a class book with new verses. Tell each pair to choose an animal name and rhyming object from the class list to create their page. Have students illustrate the verses and, when finished, let the pairs sing their new verses.

Oh, a-hunting we will go,
a-hunting we will go.
We'll catch a _____
and put it in a _____,
And then we'll let it go.

Missing Lyrics

Write the words to a very familiar song on sentence strips, omitting the rhyming words at the ends of some lines. Display the sentence strips in a pocket chart. Ask students to write the missing words on additional pieces of sentence strips and place them in the correct section of the pocket chart.

Rhyming Chants

Choose a nursery rhyme or other traditional song that has several verses, such as "This Old Man" or "Five Little Monkeys," to announce the need to change from one activity to another. Before you begin the chant, explain how to make the transition from one activity to another, and write what students should do on the board. For example, if students are moving from art time to snack time, write steps on the board such as *stand up, line up to wash hands, put brushes in the sink, get your snacks from your cubbies, sit at your seats.* (Read the directions to prereaders.) Explain that by the time the chant is finished, students should be cleaned up and sitting at their seats, ready to eat their snacks. Then, begin to chant or sing the rhyme and invite students to join in. Emphasize the rhyming words at the end of each line. When you finish the rhyme, note whether students were able to finish the transition so that you can decide whether the chant should be faster or slower next time.

Teacher's Helper: Finger Play Collection

Below are several finger plays that either repeat words or have rhyming words at the end of lines. Young students typically enjoy finger plays and tend to focus on the movement of hands and fingers. However, in the following finger plays, the emphasis should be on the rhyming words, so make sure that students know the words before learning the motions.

Finger Play: Shake Your Hands

Use the following finger play when students need to settle down. Repeat several times to "get the wiggles out."
Shake your hands and clap, clap, clap.
Shake your hands and fold them in your lap.

Finger Play: Five Fingers
I have five fingers on each hand. (Show each hand.)
I like to put them in the sand. (Wiggle all fingers.)
When I hide my thumbs just so, (Bend thumbs into palms.)
There's only four that I can show. (Show four fingers on each hand.)

Finger Play: Clap, Two, Three, Four!

Do this chant to an eight-count, with the motions on the last beat.

Clap, two, three, four, five, six, seven, eight. (Clap hands.)
Shake, two, three, four, five, six, seven, eight. (Shake fingers.)
Slap, two, three, four, five, six, seven, eight. (Slap table or knees.)
Roll, two, three, four, five, six, seven, eight. (Rotate one hand around the other.)
Snap, two, three, four, five, six, seven, eight. (Snap fingers.)
Tap, two, three, four, five, six, seven, eight. (Tap toes.)
Push, two, three, four, five, six, seven, eight. (Push hands forward.)
Clap, two, three, four, five, six, seven, eight. (Clap hands.)
Rest, two, three, four, five, six, seven, eight. (Place hands in lap.)

Finger Play: Baby Bears

Teach students to do the motions one line at a time so that they can memorize them more easily and can then focus on the rhythm.

Five baby bears in the bed; (Hold up five fingers.)
One rolled over and bumped his head. (Put hands on head.)
Four baby bears in the bed; (Hold up four fingers.)
One left to go and eat some bread. (Pretend to eat.)
Three baby bears in the bed; (Hold up three fingers.)
"I've got to go," one baby bear said. (Put hands on face.)
Two baby bears in the bed; (Hold up two fingers.)
I want my pajamas that are red! (Put hands on hips)
One baby bear in the bed; (Hold up one finger.)
He gets to have the whole bedspread! (Put hands on one side of face and pretend to go to sleep.)

Assessment of Rhyming Words

As you observe your students participating in these activities, use the reproducible form (page 50) to record your observations. For example, the activity, "A-Hunting We Will Go" presents an opportunity to document the skill of "hears and identifies rhyming pairs." Use other activities in this section to document other skills, as well as observing your students as they use these skills in other, authentic situations. Note the date and indicate any comments made by a student to support your documentation. This information can be useful during family conferences, or as you plan further lessons for your students.

Assessment for Rhyming Words

Student's name and date:	Repeats rhyme/ poem independently	Hears and identifies rhyming pairs	Names non-rhyming word in a list of words	Produces rhyming word for a prompt	Produces 3+ words when given a common rime

Consonant/Sound Correspondence

Connecting a printed symbol with a particular sound is considered a phonics skill. Phonics is the understanding that there is a predictable relationship between phonemes and graphemes, the letters that represent those sounds in written language (CIERA, 2001). Specific phonics activities are typically presented to young students only after they understand that speech is made up of separate sounds. In other words, students do not benefit from phonics instruction when they still need to develop one or more forms of phonemic awareness. This is because students who cannot hear and work with the phonemes of spoken words have difficulty learning how to relate phonemes to graphemes when they see them in written words.

Learning to connect phonemes and graphemes (sounds and letters) is a complex skill, but a strong foundation in letter/sound relationships is important to reading success (Morrow & Tracey, 1997). Not all students learn this skill in the same way, so teachers must use multiple strategies to help students learn to make these connections. For the most part, students learn a sound associated with a letter when that letter has some particular meaning for them. That is why, for most students, the first letters/sounds they learn are the first letters of their first names.

Researchers (Moustafa and Maldonado-Colon, 1999) state that the most effective instruction in letter/sound correspondence is based on two principles. It grounds instruction in letter-sound correspondences in a context that is meaningful to the student, and it builds on the spoken language students already understand rather than on letter-sound correspondences they do not yet understand. Therefore, after a student learns the first letter of his first name, he tends to learn the letters and sounds of the first names of his friends and caregivers (often, /m/ and /d/ for mom and dad). Beyond that, the order in which they learn letters varies. For example, with a student who loves soccer, s can become an early letter in his or her learning if teachers or families help the student make this connection. Therefore, early childhood educators should purposefully seek to learn each student's interests, likes, and preferences, so that they can use this information to help students make personal connections with letters/sounds.

This section offers a variety of learning experiences that help students make connections between consonants and sounds. Some activities are limited to only one letter, while other activities can be altered to teach virtually any consonant. Because the study of the alphabet naturally follows a focus on consonant sounds, some suggested alphabet activities are included at the end of this section. Also, as students learn to associate consonants with their sounds, it is natural to begin blending them with vowel sounds to make simple words. Some activities that involve associating consonants and vowels are included at the end of this section as well. Other activities that focus more directly on vowel sound activities are found in the next section.

Letter Collections

Write each consonant on a small container, such as an empty cereal box or a one-pound coffee can. Ask students to help you collect items that represent each consonant and that are small enough to fit in the boxes. For example, the box for the letter *p* might contain pennies, popcorn, paper clips, pins, pens, etc. (Make sure any food items are nonperishable and sealed in plastic bags.) When students bring in the items, enthusiastically place them in the appropriate boxes. Let the student hold up the object, then place it in the box as the class says the name of the object.

Teacher's Helper: Suggestions for Consonant Collection Boxes

The experience of locating objects for alphabet collection boxes helps students remember sounds associated with each letter of the alphabet. It is best if students are the ones who think of the objects and find them. However, this is not always possible. The lists below are suggestions for beginning these collections. Many of the objects need to be smaller versions of the real thing, such as small toy vehicles, a doll's house refrigerator, a collection of small farm and zoo animals, etc. Consider using larger containers if students would like to bring in larger items. Note that items whose names change the initial letter sound have not been listed.

B Collection Box Items
backgammon, bag, ball, balloon, banana, Band-Aids®, bandages, bar, battery, bay leaves, binoculars, bird, boat, Boggle®, bolt, boomerang, boot, bone, book, bottle, bow, bowl, box, broccoli, bubbles, bubble bath, bulb, butterfly, button, bus

Teaching Tip

Collecting small objects for the Letter Collections activity is a great family homework activity for a long holiday, such as winter or spring break. Let each student choose a letter, but enlist the help of all families with sending any appropriate objects they find to add to the collection. Many families find that the bottom of the toy box has many small, appropriate objects. Figuring out which letter each object represents reinforces understanding of letter/sound associations. Parents who shop garage sales may find objects there, but emphasize that students should be involved in finding them if possible.

C Collection Box Items

calendar, California, camel, camera, can, Canada, candle, candy, canoe, car, carpet, carrot, cashews, cat, caterpillar, cereal, circle, coconut, cocoon, Colorado, comb, computer, Connecticut, cookie, cork, corn, cow, cube, cup

D Collection Box Items

date, deer, dice, dictionary, dill, dime, dinosaur, dog, doll, dolphin, domino, doorbell, duck, Delaware

F Collection Box Items

fan, feather, finger paint, fire truck, fish, five, foil, folder, football, fork (plastic), four, fox

G Collection Box Items

gate, gel, geoboard, geode, Georgia, gerbil, giraffe, girl, globe, glue, goat, goggles, gold, golf ball, goose, gorilla, gorp, gourd, guitar, gum, gummy bears

H Collection Box Items

hair, hairpin, ham, hamburger, hamster, hammer, handkerchief, harp, hat, Hawaii, headphones, heart, helicopter, helmet, hen, hinge, hippopotamus, hole punch, horn, horse, horseshoe, hose, hot dog, hotel, house

J Collection Box Items

jacks, jaguar, jam, jar, jawbreaker, jeep, Jell-O®, jelly, jelly bean, jet, jigsaw puzzle, joey, jump rope

K Collection Box Items

kangaroo, Kansas, Kentucky, key, kite, kitten, kiwi, koala

L Collection Box Items

labels, lace, ladybug, lamb, lamp, leaf, Legos®, Lincoln Logs™, letter, lid, lion, lizard, lock, lotion, Louisiana

M Collection Box Items

magnet, mail, mailbox, Maine, man, map, marble, marker, marshmallow, Maryland, mascara, mask, Massachusetts, mayonnaise, mermaid, Michigan, microphone, Minnesota, mirror, Mississippi, Missouri, mitt, mitten, monkey, Montana, morning message, moth, motorcycle, mouse, muffins

N Collection Box Items

nail, Nebraska, needle, net, Nevada, New Hampshire, New Jersey, New Mexico, New York, newspaper, nickel, nine, Nintendo®, noodles, North Carolina, North Dakota, nut

P Collection Box Items

pan, panda, paper, parrot, parsley, patch, pattern blocks, peach, peanut, pecans, pen, pencil, pendulum, penny, penguin, Pennsylvania, pepper, peppermint, piano, pickle, pig, pillow, pink, poem, pony, poodle, popcorn, porcupine, porpoise, poster board, pot, potato, pulley, purple, puzzle

53

Q Collection Box Items
quarter, quartz, question mark, quill, quilt, Q-tips®

R Collection Box Items
rabbit, raccoon, racquetball, radio, railroad car, ramp, rat, rattle, recipe, rectangle, recycle bin, red, reel, refrigerator, reindeer, remote control, ribbon, Rhode Island, rice, ring, rock, roller skates, rooster, rope, rose, rosemary, rubber band, ruler

S Collection Box Items
saddle, sage, sail, salt, sand, sandwich, satin, seal, seed, sentence strip, sequin, sesame seeds, seven, sign, silk, six, soap, sock, South Carolina, South Dakota, sun, sunflower

T Collection Box Items
tag, tangrams, tape, taxi, tea bag, teapot, teddy bear, television, Tennessee, tennis ball, terrarium, Texas, tiger, timer, top, toothbrush, toothpaste, towel, tube, tulip, turkey

V Collection Box Items
vacuum, valentine, van, vanilla, velvet, Vermont, vest, video, violet, violin, Virginia, visor, volleyball, vulture

W Collection Box Items
wagon, Walkman®, wallpaper, wallet, walnut, walrus, wand, washcloth, Washington, wastebasket, watch, water, watermelon, West Virginia, wig, wind chimes, wire, Wisconsin, wolf, wood, Wyoming

X Collection Box Items
X-ray, xylophone

Y Collection Box Items
yacht, Yahtzee®, yak, yardstick, yarn, yellow, yo-yo

Z Collection Box Items
zebra, zero, Ziploc® bags, zipper, ziti

Extension – Make the alphabet objects even more tangible. Cut large letters out of cardboard and ask students who have not yet mastered remembering the sound of a particular letter to glue objects or pictures that begin with that letter sound onto the letter itself.

Simon Says Sounds

Play a version of Simon Says with letter sounds. Distribute index cards and announce a letter for students to write on their cards. Read a sentence that contains a word that begins with the sound of that letter. Students should stand when they hear a word that starts with that letter sound and sit if there is no word in the sentence that begins with that letter sound. For example, if the letter is *r*, read:

- The barn has a big red door. (Students stand up.)
- Roosters crow early in the morning. (Students stand up.)
- Chickens lay eggs. (Students sit down.)
- The farmer collects eggs early in the morning. (Students sit down.)

When students are capable of easily hearing the beginning sounds, play this game with ending sounds.

Teaching Tip

If students have difficulty hearing the sounds in a sentence, begin by pronouncing just the sound. For example, say /r/ as students stand up; say /b/ or /f/ as students sit down, and so on. After students have success with this, move on to pronouncing words, and then try the sentences again.

Teaching Tip

Regular-sized pillowcases may be too large for this activity. Instead, use pillowcases made for babies, or use lunch bags. If you have a parent volunteer who is willing to sew a small bag, fabric with an ABC print works well for this activity.

Feeling the Letter Sounds

Choose one consonant. Gather small objects whose names begin with that letter sound. For example, represent *c* with a cup and a toy car. Put those objects in a pillowcase, along with a few other objects whose names begin with different letter sounds. Working in pairs or small groups, have students take turns using their sense of touch to find objects that begin with the targeted letter sound.

Last Letter First

Complete this activity if you have a word wall in your classroom. When the word wall has multiple words under each consonant, teach small groups of students to play "Last Letter First." Have a student read a word from the word wall. The next student should take the last letter of that word and read another word from the word wall that begins with that letter, and so on.

Extension – As students become accomplished at remembering the sounds associated with all of the letters, challenge them to play the game in a circle. The first student should say any word that comes to mind. The next student should say the final sound of that word and then say a new word with that same sound as the initial sound, and so on. Remind students that they are to use the final sound they hear, not the final letter of the correctly spelled word. For example, the game might go as follows: book, kite, table, leaf, fog, goat, etc.

Dogs and Bones: Initial /m/ and /n/

Enlarge and cut out the bone patterns, directions, and answer key box (page 57). Copy the dog patterns on colorful paper, or copy them on white paper and color the patterns. Cut out the dog patterns. Glue the directions to the front of a file folder. Glue the dog named Manny to one inside flap of the file folder, and the dog named Nanny to the other inside flap. Gather old magazines or other resources for pictures. Have students go on a scavenger hunt to find small pictures of objects that begin with the letters *m* and *n*. Cut out the pictures and glue each to half of a small index card. Glue a bone next to each picture. Write the picture names on the answer key. Store the bone cards and answer key in a resealable, plastic bag. Read the directions to individual students as they play the game by matching the pictures with the /m/ and /n/ sounds. Help students check their work.

Teaching Tip

Constructing file folder games that follow basically the same directions helps students remember how to play them. Put directions in the same place on the front of each folder. Glue small paper pockets, such as library card pockets, or tape resealable plastic bags to the backs of folders to hold game pieces. (Make a small hole in the bag so it does not trap air.) Before students play the games, demonstrate how to read the directions, remove and store the pieces, be gentle with the folders, and replace them when finished. Other possible combinations for games similar to dogs and bones include squirrels and nuts, chickens and eggs, Dalmatians and spots, a beehive and bees, etc. Leftover phonics workbooks, housewares catalogs, and sticker packs are good sources for pictures.

Dogs and Bones: Initial /m/ and /n/

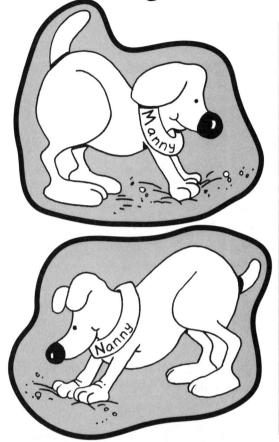

Directions:

Manny and Nanny buried all of their bones in the same pile. Manny likes pictures of words that start with the /m/ sound. Nanny likes pictures of words that start with the /n/ sound. Can you help them find their own pictures? Place all of the pictures in the same pile. Then, choose a picture, say the word, listen for the first sound, and place it beside the right dog.

Answer Key:

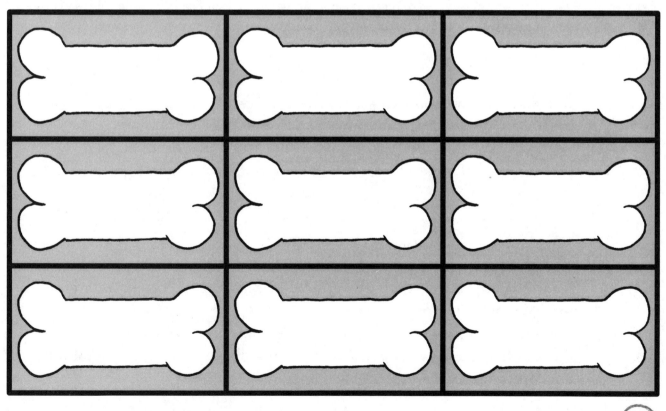

Nodding Heads

Use this game to compare different concepts, such as initial or final sounds or medial vowels. Say several pairs of words. Ask students to nod "yes" if the words in a pair have the same initial sound, or shake their heads "no" if the sounds are different. Students can also show finger spelling signs: *y* for yes or *n* for no (page 30), or "thumbs up" and "thumbs down." When students master this activity, say three words to increase difficulty.

Animal Bingo

Copy the Bingo Grid and animals (pages 59–60) for each student. Review the animals' names. (Animal names are *bear, cat, dog, fish, goat, horse, jellyfish, kangaroo, lion, monkey, newt, pig, quail, rabbit, sea horse, tiger, vulture, walrus, yak,* and *zebra.* Note that some of these pictures and those on subsequent pages may be unfamiliar to students. Either review the pictures with students or eliminate pictures you do not want to use.) To complete the game boards, let each student cut out nine animals and paste them in the grid spaces. To play the game, say a beginning sound of one animal's name. When a student finds a corresponding picture, she should place a marker on it. The first student to get three in a row is the winner.

Extension – Use the food and object pictures (pages 61–64) as well as magazine pictures and children's sticker books to create new Bingo games. See the teaching tip below for directions about how to create more card sets. (Food names are *banana, corn, doughnut, fish, gingerbread, hamburger, ice cream, jam, kiwi, lemons, milk, nuts, peas, raisins, salad, tomato, vegetables, watermelon,* and *zucchini.* Object names are *bed, curtains, desk, fan, gate, house, jacks, kite, lamp, moon, nest, pin, queen, ribbon, sun, tape, van, window, xylophone, yarn,* and *zipper.*)

Teaching Tip

To create your own class Bingo set that is relevant to your phonics program, draw the template using a computer drawing program. Then, locate clip art and electronically cut and paste it into copies of the cards. Print out the cards, cut them out, and laminate them for durability.

Teaching Tip

When students begin to use the additional pictures you have created for Animal Bingo, limit picture choices to familiar beginning sounds. When students are proficient with these, let them mix and match all of the pictures to make new cards. Make sure students know that they must use only one picture to represent each beginning sound.

Bingo Grid

Animal Bingo Pictures

Animal/Food Bingo Pictures

Food/Object Bingo Pictures

Let's Play Ball: Initial /b/ and /f/

Copy and color the mice, bats, directions and answer key (page 66), and cut out the patterns. Glue the directions to the front of a file folder, and store the bats and answer key in a resealable, plastic bag. Glue Billy Mouse to one side of the inside of the folder and glue Filly Mouse to the other. (You will need to read the directions to the players and show them how to take turns.) If desired, write additional words on copies of the blank bat patterns, then show students how to mix up the patterns and turn them facedown. Let pairs play the game to learn the /b/ and /f/ sounds. Encourage students to check each other's work, reminding them to emphasize the /b/ or /f/ so that they reinforce those sounds for each other.

Grab the Letter

Write letters on small index cards and put them in a paper bag. For variety, include a "Pass" card that allows a free turn or a "Draw Again" card that gives the student two turns in a row. Ask a student to reach into the bag, take out a letter, and say the letter and the sound that matches the letter. If she is correct, let her keep the card. If she is incorrect, she must put the card back in the bag. The student with the most cards at the end of the game is the winner.

Search for Sounds

Before beginning this activity, create a bulletin board or chart titled "The ABCs of Our School." Focus on a different letter each day. Leave space for students to write or draw objects. As you are walking in the hall, challenge students to find something that begins with a particular sound. For example, if the sound is /b/, students might notice a bulletin board, ball, or brick. When you return to class, ask the student who first noticed the object to add it to the chart.

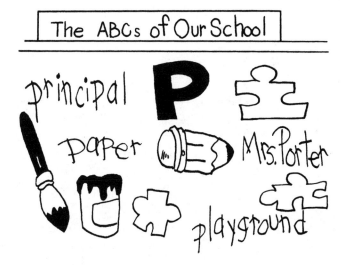

Pick a Fist

Display several letters on a table and make sure students can identify them. Then, put the letters in a small container so students cannot see them. Choose two letters and hide one in each hand. First, let a student "pick a fist." Then, as you display it, have him say the letter and its sound. If correct, the student gets to keep the letter; if incorrect, it goes back into the container. When all letters have been chosen, let each student who participated write the letters he kept on a piece of paper.

Let's Play Ball: Initial /b/ and /f/

Directions: Help Billy and Filly play ball. Billy uses bats with words that begin with the /b/ sound. Filly uses bats with words that begin with the /f/ sound. Turn over the bats. The first player should draw one bat and read the word on the bat aloud. The second player should name the first sound in the word and place the bat next to the correct mouse. If the player is correct, he or she keeps the bat and it is the next player's turn. If a player is incorrect, the bat goes back into the pile. Play until all bats are used.

Answer Key:
Billy's bats are bag, bet, bit, boat, bud.
Filly's bats are fact, fell, fish, foot, fun.

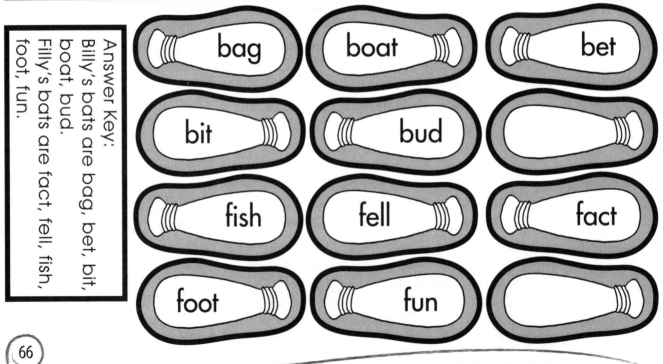

bag boat bet

bit bud

fish fell fact

foot fun

Let's Go Shopping

Give each student food magazines, grocery store ads or coupon circulars, scissors, and a small paper bag. Point out pictures of foods. If the student can name the initial sound in the name of each food, he should cut it out and place it in his "grocery bag." The winner is the student with the most "groceries" in the "grocery bag." When the game is over, ask students to "put away the groceries" by placing all of the pictures on the table and reviewing the initial sound of each.

POW!

To review letter sounds with a small group of students, write the letters associated with those sounds on index cards. Also write the word POW! on several cards. Put all cards into a paper bag. Gather students in a circle so that passing the bag is easy. Let each student select one card. If she can pronounce the sound, she should keep the card and pass the bag to the left. If she cannot pronounce the sound, everyone in the group should remind her, and she should then place the card back into the bag and pass it. If a student pulls out a POW! card, she must say "POW!" and put all of her cards back into the bag. The student with the most cards at the end of the game is the winner.

Letter Search

On several index cards, write words that begin (or end) with the same letter. For example, when focusing on the letter *f*, distribute cards that have words with *f* as the first letter (*fish, farm, feather, fold, family, fun, find, feed*), as the last letter (*leaf, wolf, relief, elf, self, beef*), and somewhere in the word but not the first or last letter (*before, after, refill, awful, beautiful, unfair*). Also, use words that have two *f*'s somewhere in the word (*cuff, raffle, baffle, taffy*), with an *r* after the *f* (*fruit, frog, free, fruit, friend, fresh*), and with an *l* after it (*flag, flood, fly, flash, flip, floor*). Distribute one card to each student. Ask students to display their words in response to your questions, such as "If you have a word with *f* as the first letter, place it in the pocket chart."

Teaching Tip

Store the cards from Letter Search in resealable, plastic bags. Label each bag with the letter. Include a list of the questions.

●●● Writing the Sound

This brief focus on individual letter sounds reinforces what students already know. It also gives a quick assessment of letter sounds that individual students need to spend more time on. Spend one minute of small group instruction dictating sounds students have learned. Have them write the letter or letters associated with each sound. Collect the papers and use them to identify which sounds need to be retaught.

Extension – Have students work in groups of three, with one proficient student acting in the role of "letter sound caller" and two others writing the letter for the sounds they hear. Provide the "caller" with a list of about 10 letter sounds to use.

Teacher's Helper: Tasting Experiences for Remembering Consonant Sounds

Students who are experiencing difficulty hearing or remembering the sounds of different letters often benefit from being able to connect a specific word to each letter. Active experiences, such as eating, often help students remember a word and therefore its beginning letter sound. Below are several suggestions of foods to represent each consonant of the alphabet. Be sure to consider brand name products, as well, since these add more variety and are often familiar to students.

B - bananas, bagels, beans, beets, biscuits, burritos, butter, butterscotch
C - carrots, cabbage, cantaloupe, cashews, cauliflower, coleslaw, cookies, corn, cucumber, cupcakes
D - doughnuts, dates, dip (for vegetables)
F - fajitas, falafel, fish, fig

Teaching Tip

Change the writing medium used in the Writing the Sound activity. Consider providing sand in shallow boxes (shoe box lids work well), paintbrushes with paint or water and construction paper, large paintbrushes to use with water on the chalkboard, etc.

Teaching Tip

When planning a food activity, be sure to get parental permission and check for food allergies and religious and other preferences.

G – garlic bread, gum

H – ham, hamburger, honey, honeydew melon, hot dogs, hummus

J – jam, Jell-O®, jelly, jelly beans, juice

K – kale, kielbasa, kiwi, knish, kumquat, kohlrabi

L – lasagna, lemon, lemonade, lettuce, licorice, lime

M – macaroni, mango, marshmallows, matzo, meatballs, melba toast, milk, mushrooms

N – nachos, nectarine, noodles, nuts

P – pancakes, papaya, peaches, peanuts, peanut butter, pears, peppers, pecans, pickles, pineapple, pizza, popcorn, potato, pumpkin

Q – quesadilla, quiche, quinces

R – radicchio, raisins, raspberries, ravioli, rice, rolls, rutabaga

S – sandwiches, sesame seeds, squash, sunflower seeds, sushi

T – tabbouleh, tacos, taffy, tangerine, tea, tofu, tomatoes, tortillas, tuna, turkey, turnips

V – vanilla pudding, vanilla wafers, vegetables, vegetable soup

W – waffles, walnuts, watercress, watermelon

X – X-crackers (narrow slices of cheese placed on a cracker in the shape of an X), Chex® cereal

Y – yams, yogurt

Z – ziti, zucchini, Zwieback® toast

Extension – Using pictures from seed catalogs, grocery circulars, and coupons, have students create a food poster for each letter of the alphabet.

Extension – Introduce the book *Eating the Alphabet* by Lois Ehlert (Harcourt, 1994) to reinforce tasting experiences involving fruits and vegetables.

Potluck Stew Letters

After students have had multiple experiences tasting foods that begin with consonants, enlarge the cooking pot (right) on gray construction paper. Encourage students to take turns creating a "potluck stew" of letters they can recognize. Turn a set of letter cards facedown in the middle of the table. Let a student select a card and say the letter and its sound. If the student is correct, the letter card is placed "in" the stew pot. If incorrect, the card is returned to the pile.

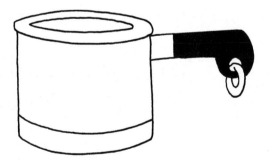

Bouncing Balls

Obtain a supply of rubber balls (available at party supply stores). Give one to each student. Take students outside or to a room where they can bounce the balls safely. When you say a /b/ word, every student should bounce his ball. When you say a word that does not begin with the /b/ sound, students should remain still.

Do This!: D Action Words

Gather students together and explain that you will play a game during which they must listen very carefully. Model the actions you want them to use for each /d/ action you plan to use. Instead of just calling out the word, tell students to "do this" or "don't do this." If you say "don't do this," students should continue doing the previous action. If a student changes actions, he must stop playing and sit down. The last student playing is the winner. Action words could be *dance, dash, dive, dry off*, etc. So, for example, call out, "Don't dance!" or "Do dry off!" and see who follows /d/ directions.

Friendly Fun: Pretending F Actions

Explain that "friends" often do things together. Ask each student to pair with a friend and pretend to do things that begin with the letter *f*. Emphasize the /f/ sound as you tell students to fan themselves, feed a pet, fidget, file their nails, go fishing, fix a machine, fold paper, and play football. (If a student questions the blend at the beginning of the word "friend," explain that even though it is a blend, the /f/ sound is still at the beginning of the word, and note that none of the actions start with blends.)

Go, Go: G Action Words

Discuss several action words that begin with the letter *g*, such as *gallop, gasp, get, give, glare, glide, glimpse,* and *go.* Demonstrate the behavior for any words students do not know, then challenge them to listen very carefully and change what they are doing as you call out different words.

Happy Hikers: H Action Words

Discuss action words that begin with the letter *h*, such as *hike, hip-hop, hiss, hold, holler, hop, hug, hum,* and shouting *hooray.* Demonstrate the behavior for words students do not know. Lead students as they pretend to hike around the room, quickly changing their movements as you call out different words.

Jumping Jacks: J Action Words

Teach students how to do jumping jacks. Have them shout "J" when their hands meet above their heads and call out /j/ when their hands come back down to touch their thighs.

Licking Lollipops: L Action Words

Discuss action words that begin with the letter *l*, such as *laugh, lean, leave, liftoff, limp, lock, look,* and *lunge.* Demonstrate behavior for any words students do not know. Ask students to hold pretend lollipops as they demonstrate the actions you say.

Moving and Mimicking: M Action Words

Discuss action words that begin with the letter *m*, such as *march in a marching band; measure and mix ingredients; mend clothes; move; mimic; mime; motion for someone to come closer; move like a monkey, a mouse, a moose, or a mole;* and *make a (pretend) mess.* Ask students to mimic actions as you say them. Encourage them to quickly change activities. Emphasize the /m/ sound each time you tell students what to pretend.

No No No!: N Action Words

Take students to a place where they can make some noise. Ask several yes-or-no questions, some serious and some silly. When you ask a serious question, such as, "Is today Wednesday?" have students nod their heads. When you ask a silly question, such as, "Can a pig drive a car?" let students shout, "No!"

Picking Pansies: P Action Words

Discuss action words that begin with the letter *p*, such as *pack, pant, peel, pick, pinch, pitch,* and *pose.* Demonstrate the behavior for any words students do not know. Have students pretend to pick (or plant) pansies (or peonies, petunias, potatoes, etc.), peel a pear, pose for a picture, etc. If possible, provide pictures of the actions.

Quick, Quack!: Q Action Words

Discuss several action words that begin with the letter *q*, such as *quack like a duck, walk like a queen, be quiet,* and *quiver.* Demonstrate the behavior for any words students do not know. Have students pretend do these actions. Say, "Quickly!" to encourage them to move faster, and "Quit!" when you want them to do a new action.

Ready Runners: R Action Words

Discuss action words that begin with the letter *r*, such as *ram, rap, rattle, reach, read, recite, record, rest, roar, roll, romp, row, rub,* and *run.* Demonstrate behavior for any words students do not know. Have students pretend to be at the starting gate for a race. As you call out different action words, they should change their behavior from "ready" to the action. Students should return to the "ready" position when you call out, "Ready!"

Silly Slow Steps: S Action Words

Ask students to move in "slow motion" to do things in a "silly" way, such as *saw wood, search for a lost object, sew, sing a song, sip soda, sit, ski,* or *stir.* Students may exaggerate their movements. For example, as students "search for a lost object," they may look high and low, bending and stretching. Emphasize the /s/ sound each time you tell students what to pretend.

Too Tired: T Action Words

Discuss several action words that begin with the letter *t,* such as *take, talk, tell, tickle, tiptoe,* and *topple.* Demonstrate the behavior for any words students do not know. Pretend to do these actions with students. When you call out, "Too tired!" students should sit or lie on the floor and pretend to be tired.

Walking Wanderers: W Action Words

Discuss several action words that begin with the letter *w,* such as *waddle, wag, wait, wake, walk, wander, wash, wave,* and *weave.* Demonstrate the behavior for any words students do not know. Suggest that students should wander around the room as they demonstrate the actions you call out.

Yelling: Y Words

Write a large uppercase and lowercase *y* on poster board. Take students and the poster outside to a place where students can be loud. Tell students that you will yell a word that begins with the letter *y,* such as *yahoo, yak, yay, yeah, yellow, yes, yippee, yoo-hoo,* or *yuck.* Then, raise the "Y" poster to prompt students to yell that word and raise their arms so that their bodies form a y-shape. Vary the activity by instructing students to only yell words that start with the letter *y.* Next, yell a word that does not start with *y.*

Zap Freeze: Z Action Words

Take students outside where there is room to run. Start in the "freeze" position. Call out different actions that begin with the /z/ sound, such as *zip, zoom,* and *zigzag.* Emphasize the /z/ sound for each action. Between each action, say, "Zap!" Have students freeze (stand motionless) when they hear that word.

Letter Sound Concentration

Write each alphabet letter on two index cards. Place cards facedown on a table in a grid. Have students take turns turning over two cards at a time. If the letters on them do not match, the student should turn the cards facedown again. If the cards match and the student can say the letter sound, the student can keep the cards. After one turn, the next student takes a turn. To simplify the game, play with smaller letter sets.

72

Twist and Shout

Draw a large circle on the board at students' eye-level. Divide it into wedges and write one letter students are studying in each section. Have a student stand in front of the board with her back turned. Chant the following rhyme with her, then instruct her to turn around during the last line of the chant, point to a letter, and say the sound associated with that letter. If desired, have students do motions with the poem, such as twisting during the first line, dancing during the second line, and spinning during the third line, so that they will be more spontaneous when they get to turn around and point to a letter.

"Twist and shout,
Rock it out.
Turn this way,
So I can say . . . ."

What's the Sound?

Sing this song for any letter sound to the tune of "Old MacDonald." This example is for the letter *b*.

What's the sound that starts these words?
Bubble, bear, and bike.
/b/ is the sound that starts these words:
Bubble, bear, and bike.
With a /b/, /b/ here and a /b/, /b/ there,
Here a /b/, there a /b/, everywhere a /b/, /b/.
/b/ is the sound that starts these words:
Bubble, bear, and bike.

> ### Teaching Tip
> This song can also be sung to locate ending sounds. Just change the lyrics accordingly.

Hello, Hello

Use this rhyme as part of the morning message to let students know it is time to begin the day. Emphasize the /h/ sound in *hello, how, hope,* and *hola* as you teach the following rhyme in English and Spanish. (Note for native English speakers that the Spanish *h* is silent.)

Hello, hello
Hello, and how are you?
I'm fine, I'm fine,
And I hope that you are, too.

Hola, hola
¿Hola y cómo estas?
Estoy bien, estoy bien,
Espero que tu tambien.

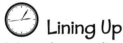 ## The Zookeeper at the Zoo

Ask students to brainstorm names of animals they might see at a zoo. Sing the song below to the tune of "The Farmer in the Dell," and let students know at what point to insert the animal names. When singing the song, emphasize the /z/ sounds of *zookeeper* and *zoo*. To make the song funnier, change the word *fed* to different verbs, such as *washed, tickled,* etc.

The (zebra) at the zoo,
The (zebra) at the zoo,
Is fed by the zookeeper,
The (zebra) at the zoo.

Lining Up

Ask students to line up by a particular letter sound. For example, say, "If your name starts with an /n/ sound, line up; if your name has a /b/ sound anywhere, line up," etc. Say the sounds in either random or alphabetical order, making sure to include vowel sounds and digraphs. To make the activity more challenging, call out some sounds to which no names correspond.

Move and Dance, then Freeze!

Insert an active minute between passive learning experiences by changing the rules of this traditional activity. Have students listen for initial consonant sounds. Announce a letter sound and tell students that as long as you say words that begin with that letter sound, they can dance (quietly, so that they can hear the words). When they hear a word that begins with a different letter sound, they must freeze. For example, if the sound is /b/, students can dance while you say words such as *bat, boat, beach, bathtub, book, butter,* and *bee.* As soon as they hear a word that begins with a different sound, such as *food,* they should freeze. Let one of the "freezers" choose the next initial consonant sound to use.

Extension – Play this activity with any feature of phonemic awareness or phonics. Instead of initial consonant sounds, feature initial vowel sounds, rhyming words, ending sounds of words, or even medial sounds.

I Spy

Play the traditional I Spy game with one exception: Start every description with the sentence, "I spy something that starts with the _____ sound."

Teacher's Helper: More Finger Plays

Many teachers use finger plays as a concrete way for students to associate sounds and letters. Use this collection of finger plays (some of which appear earlier in this book) during transition times, in small groups, or with individual students. The various finger plays emphasize different sounds, and the rhythm and rhyme help students pay attention to language.

Finger Play: Five Fingers (/f/)
I have five fingers on each hand. (Show each hand.)
I like to put them in the sand. (Wiggle all fingers.)
When I hide my thumb just so, (Bend thumbs back.)
There's only four that I can show. (Show four fingers on each hand.)

Finger Play: Pairs (For this rhyme, tell students which initial sound to listen for, and have them raise their hands when they hear it. Possible sounds include /p/, /t/, /h/, and /m/.)

Two things make a pair. (Hold up two fingers.)
And on me, I'll show you where. (Point to self.)
I have two ears, and I have two eyes. (Point to ears and eyes.)
Both are important to make me wise! (Scratch head as if thinking.)

I have two holes in my nose. (Point to nose.)
That lets me smell a beautiful rose. (Pretend to smell a rose.)
I have two hands that clap a beat. (Clap hands twice.)
I have two feet that are really neat! (Jump when saying the word *neat*.)

Finger Play: Five Merry Monkeys Jumping on the Bed (/m/)
Five merry monkeys jumping on the bed. (Raise five fingers and bounce hand to the rhythm of the verse.)
One fell off and bumped his head. (Hold up one finger, then rub head.)
Mommy called the doctor and the doctor said, (Hold hand to ear like a phone.)
"NO MORE MONKEYS JUMPING ON THE BED!" (Shake index finger.)
Continue with four, three, two, etc., repeating gestures appropriately.

Finger Play: Five Funny Frogs (/f/)
Five funny friendly frogs
Sitting on a fuzzy log
Eating some most fantastic bugs.
Yum Yum!
(Pretend to catch bugs.)
One flopped into the pool
(Pretend to jump in a pond.)
Where it was fresh and cool
Now there are four friendly frogs.
Glub, glub!

Continue with four, three, etc.

Finger Play: Five Little Tadpoles (/s/ as an initial and ending consonant)
Seven little tadpoles swimming near the shore,
The first one said, "Let's swim some more."
(Put palms together; make swimming movements.)
The second one said, "Let's rest awhile."
(Rest hands on knees.)
The third one said, "Swimming makes me smile."
(Point to smile.)
The fourth one said, "My legs are growing long."
(Stretch legs straight.)
The fifth one said, "I'm getting very strong."
(Make fists and show muscles.)
The sixth one said, "Let's breathe some air."
(Take a deep breath.)
The seventh one said, "Let's look up there!
(Look up as if looking out of the water.)
Seven little tadpoles will soon be frogs,
They'll jump from the water and sit on logs.

Erase the Alphabet

In random order, write the letters of the alphabet on the board. Have a small group of students take turns saying the sounds of the letters in alphabetic order. Erase each letter as it is said. To make the activity more challenging, have students erase the letters themselves, or have students say the letter sounds in order without first writing them on the board, and then write the letters as they are said.

Letter Posters

Assign students to small groups. Give each group catalogs, scissors, glue, and a poster board labeled with a consonant. Challenge each group to find pictures of objects that begin with the consonant sound represented by the letter on their poster. Have groups share their posters with the whole class.

Extension – Encourage families to make an ABC book at home. Ask parents to create a book of 26 blank pages and let their children write a letter on each page. Suggest cutting pictures from magazines, newspapers, or grocery circulars. If some parents do not have these items, suggest that they help their children think of objects for each letter of the alphabet to draw or paint.

Egg Carton Letters

Cut off the lids of two empty dozen-sized egg cartons. Cut off three cups from the second carton and staple the remaining nine-cup section to the end of the other carton to make 21 spaces, one for each consonant. In alphabetical order, write one consonant on the side of each egg cup. Give the cartons to a small group. Say a sound and ask students to put a small marker in that cup. Repeat with several other sounds, checking each time to see that students have identified the correct sound. Vary the game by asking students to say a word that starts with the sound before moving the marker or to match letters with the letter name you say.

Teaching Tip

If seeing all of the letters at one time is too confusing, cut the cartons in half to make spaces for six letters at a time. Make several of these, varying the letters that are in each group. (Include one with only short vowels, as well.) If egg cartons are not available, use ice cube trays.

Teacher's Helper: Alphabet Books

While there are many alphabet books, the following selection suggests books that are particularly appealing to young students or that incorporate an unusual idea or concept. Challenge students to compare alphabet books to see the similarities and differences in them.

26 Letters and 99 Cents by Tana Hoban (Greenwillow, 1987)
In colorful, striking photographs, Hoban depicts a few different objects for each letter. Turning the book upside down reveals a totally different book about money.

A is for Salad by Mike Lester (Grosset & Dunlap, 2000)
Study the illustrations to figure out what each letter really stands for. It is obvious that A stands for the alligator who is eating the salad, but not all letters are that easily identified.

A My Name is Alice by Jane Bayer (Puffin, 1987)
Bayer uses the jump rope chant to create short, rhythmic rhymes based on the letters of the alphabet and animals from around the world. Steven Kellogg's whimsical illustrations support the rhymes.

Action Alphabet by Shelley Rotner (Atheneum, 1996)
Students of different ages, genders, and ethnicities are shown in action (for example, arching, blowing, climbing) in crisp, colorful photographs.

Albert's Alphabet by Leslie Tyron (Aladdin, 1994)
Albert the duck is challenged by the principal of the school where he works as a carpenter to "build the alphabet" for the school in one day. Albert uses found objects to create all 26 letters before his deadline.

Alligators All Around: An Alphabet by Maurice Sendak (HarperTrophy, 1991)
Sendak's illustrations show alligators doing all sorts of things except napping. (Alligators "never nap.")

Alligator Arrived with Apples: A Potluck Alphabet Feast by Crescent Dragonwagon (Aladdin, 1992)
Dragonwagon's alliterative alphabet story describes a most unusual Thanksgiving feast. There is Elderberry Elixir from Elephant, Mocha Mousse made by Mouse, and Zebra's Zaftig Zucchini.

Alphabatics by Suse MacDonald (Simon & Schuster, 1986)
This Caldecott winner devotes a full spread to each letter, showing the letter in uppercase and lowercase, a few transformations from the letter itself to part of the illustration of an animal, the name of the animal, and a cut-paper illustration of that animal.

Alphabet City by Stephen T. Johnson (Puffin, 1999)
This book first appears to be photographs of city scenes where letters are found in everyday places. But, the illustrations are created with pastels, watercolors, gouache, and charcoal. The letters can be hard to identify, but the creativity and beautiful paintings make this alphabet book worth reading.

The Alphabet From Z to A (With Much Confusion on the Way) by Judith Viorst (Atheneum, 1994)
Viorst offers a more sophisticated look at letters and their sounds in this "backwards" alphabet book.

Alphabet Under Construction by Denise Fleming (Henry Holt and Company, 2002)
Fleming shows a mouse character constructing the alphabet—airbrushing the A, buttoning the B, carving the C, etc., using all kinds of tools, ladders, and scaffolds.

Alpha-Blocks by Kat Anderson (Longstreet Press, 1993)
Using cartoon pictures of objects that begin with each letter of the alphabet, Anderson's puzzle-type book shows matching sounds and letters. A mix of obvious and challenging sounds makes a fun read.

Animal Action ABC by Karen Pandell (Dutton Children's Books, 1996)
For each letter of the alphabet, Pandell selects an action word (*arch, balance, charge, drink,* etc.) and writes a poem that begins with that word. Photographs show animals and students "doing" each action.

Animal Parade: A Wildlife Alphabet by Jakki Wood (Sagebrush, 1999)
Wood features each letter of the alphabet in paintings of 98 different animals.

Arches to Zigzags: An Architecture ABC by Michael J. Crosbie (Harry N. Abrams, 2000)
Colorful photographs taken in many different states depict architectural forms and functions. Brief rhymes accompany each photograph.

The Butterfly Alphabet by Kjell B. Sandved (Scholastic, 1999)
It took Sandved over 25 years and visits to 30 countries to find 26 butterflies and moths, each with the likeness of one letter on its wings. Photographs show each entire butterfly and a close-up of the letter.

Children from Australia to Zimbabwe: A Photographic Journey Around the World by Maya Ajmera and Anna Rhesa Versola (Charlesbridge, 2001)
This book includes facts about 25 different countries (the imaginary country of Xanadu represents "X"), but the beautiful photographs of each country's children are the major strength of this book.

Community Helpers from A to Z by Bobbie Kalman (Crabtree Publishing, 1997)
Diverse photographs and descriptions depict each community helper. It includes unusual helpers, such as an emergency medical technician, a gymnastics coach, a utility worker, and a water treatment worker.

Dr. Seuss's ABC: An Amazing Book! by Dr. Seuss (Random House, 1996)
Beginning with Aunt Annie's Alligator and ending with Zizzer-Zazzer-Zuzz, Dr. Seuss uses the alphabet to introduce new comical creatures, each with its own alliterative rhyme.

Eating the Alphabet: Fruits and Vegetables from A to Z by Lois Ehlert (Harcourt, 1994)
Ehlert offers a watercolored fruit and vegetable for each letter of the alphabet. A glossary tells each food's origin and how it is eaten or where it is grown.

Everyday Structures from A to Z by Bobbie Kalman (Crabtree Publishing, 2000)
Using a combination of photographs, drawings, and paintings, this book depicts terms related to natural or man-made structures. It offers a paragraph-long explanation of each term.

Farm Alphabet Book by Jane Miller (Scholastic, 1987)
Each letter of the alphabet is portrayed with a color photograph, the uppercase and lowercase letter, one word, and a sentence or two about the farm-related photograph.

From Acorn to Zoo and Everything in Between in Alphabetical Order by Satoshi Kitamura (Farrar, Straus & Giroux, 1995)
Using paper cutouts to illustrate several objects for each letter of the alphabet, Kitamura also labels each object and poses an alliterative question. This book expands students' vocabularies and their observation skills.

The Ocean Alphabet Book by Jerry Pallotta (Charlesbridge Publishing, 1986)
In *The Ocean Alphabet Book*, Frank Mazzola's detailed illustrations strongly support Pallotta's informational paragraphs about 26 different ocean-related animals.

On Market Street by Arnold Lobel (Greenwillow, 1981)
At first glance, this is the story of a little boy who buys something that begins with each letter of the alphabet. However, this book is unique because the shopkeepers are created from what they are selling; the apple vendor is made of apples; the bookseller is made of books, and so on.

Tomorrow's Alphabet by George Shannon (HarperTrophy, 1999)
This book is for students who have mastered the letter sequence of the alphabet. At first, it appears confusing when the first page contends that A is for seed. Turning the page, the books explains, a seed is "tomorrow's apple." The book challenges the reader to predict what letters really represent.

Wildflower ABC: An Alphabet of Potato Prints by Diana Pomeroy (Harcourt, 1997)
This beautiful book of flower art uses potatoes to create the intricate prints of some familiar plants, such as columbine and dandelion, as well as more obscure plants, like wally basket and xerophyllum tenax.

The Z Was Zapped: A Play in Twenty-Six Acts by Chris Van Allsburg (Houghton Mifflin, 1987)
Each letter of the alphabet is on stage, and is undergoing a dramatic transformation. Relevant text is on the back of the illustrations, which allows students to guess what is happening to each letter.

Alphabet Books on Tape
Tape record a favorite alphabet book. Read the text for each page, then say the letter sound and ask students to write the corresponding letter. Let students work through a few pages at a time that correlate to letters they are learning.

Extension - After students know most of the letter sounds, record the entire book, with directions at the end of the tape. For example, say, "Find the page that shows the /f/ sound. Check with your partner to make sure you found the same page." Repeat similar directions for other letters.

Creating Class-Made Alphabet Books
Suggest several possible topics for class-made alphabet books, such as zoo animals, plants, foods, etc. Have students sign up for books they wish to work on, then research their topics by looking at alphabet books, brainstorming with friends, etc. Then, instruct students to draw a page for each letter, using crayons, markers, or a computer drawing program. Let students think of creative ways to bind their books. For example, they could use colorful yarn that matches a book's theme or illustration, such as black and white like a zebra in an animal book, or natural materials like twigs and raffia in a plant book.

Extension - Organizing ABC information can be challenging for young students. Distribute copies of the Alphabetical Order reproducible (page 81). Then, instruct students to draw (or write) the object beside the letter on the list. Students can see at a glance what letters are missing.

The Alphabet Song
Sing "The Alphabet Song" to get students' attention. Set this up as a routine; when students hear that song, they should stop what they are doing, face you, and join in. After students have sung "The Alphabet Song" many times, change the way you sing it by using letter sounds instead of letter names.

A	B	C
D	E	F
G	H	I
J	K	L
M	N	O
P	Q	R
S	T	U
V	W	X
Y	Z	

Letter Boards

First, make simple letter display boards. Cut poster board or card stock in 8^1/$_2$" x 11" rectangles. For each board, cut two 1^1/$_2$" x 11" strips from an overhead transparency or other heavy, clear plastic. Use clear tape to tape the bottom of one strip to the middle of the board, and the bottom of the other strip to the bottom of the board, to form pockets to hold the letter cards. Assign students to small groups and give each student his own board. (Allow different groups to meet at different times to limit the number of letter boards you have to make.) Cut 3" x 5" index cards in half to create 1^1/$_2$" x 2^1/$_2$" cards. Give each student four to six cards. Tell students which letters to write on their cards. For example, say, "Write A on your first card, B on your second card, C on your third card, and T on your last card." Then, when you say each sound, students should place the correct letter card on their letter boards. Using the letters in the example, say:

- Show me /a/.
- Show me /t/.
- Show me /c/.
- Show me /b/.
- Show me the letters that make the word /a/ - /t/.
- Show me the letters that make the word /b/ - /a/ - /t/.
- Show me the letters that make the word /c/ - /a/ - /t/.
- Show me the letters that make the word /c/ - /a/ - /b/.

> ## Teaching Tip
>
> If you cannot use plastic to make the pockets for the letter boards, sentence strips will work, but keep in mind that these are opaque and may cut off the bottoms of the letters. You can also use a pocket chart or clear photo pockets for this activity.

Word Sort

Write 15–20 simple words on large index cards and place them in a pocket chart. Tell students how to sort the words into different categories, such as those that begin with a certain sound, have a certain vowel sound, contain a certain blend or end with a particular letter, etc. Have students sort the words into different piles. As students become proficient in this activity, challenge them to discover other attributes that the words have in common, and sort by those characteristics.

Word Ladders

Assign students to small groups. Provide letter tiles and the Word Ladder reproducible (page 84) to each group. Ask students to find the letters to spell a word they know, then challenge them to add or remove letters to build other words, creating a ladder of words. Model this activity several times before having students build word ladders on their own. Three possible examples of word ladders are:

at	do	car
hat	dog	care
cat	dig	cake
rat	big	make
rate	bit	lake

Letter Roll

Create sets of letter dice for this activity by writing a letter on each side of a small block, blank die, or blank inflatable cube, repeating letters as needed. Or, write letters on small stickers if you want to change them easily. (If you are working with particular letters, create dice that contain only those letters.) Store the letter dice in resealable, plastic bags for students to use in small groups. Ask a student to roll a letter die, look at the word wall or a list of words, and say a word from the word wall or word list that begins with that letter.

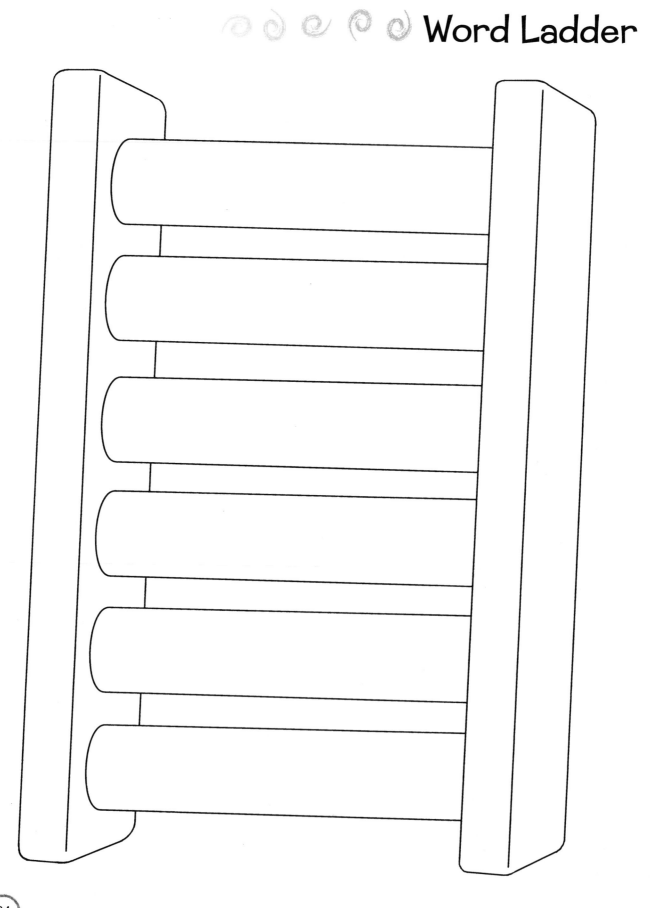

The Name Museum

Designate one corner of the classroom as a "museum." On a table, display the first letter of each student's name. (To acquire letters, check local craft stores or home centers for large, decorative wooden or plaster letters. If these are not available, use a decorative font to make unusual forms of the letters, and copy them on colorful paper.) Then, ask each student to find an object(s) whose name begins with the same letter sound as his name. For example, Mark might place a marker or some dried macaroni beside his "M," Jacque might put a box of Jell-O® or jumping beans near her "J," etc. Maintain the museum for several weeks, challenging each student to add an alphabetically appropriate object each week.

Teaching Tip

Decide ahead of time how to deal with students' names that begin with letters that do not correspond to the usual sounds, such as the J in Joaquin. Since this lesson focuses on letter recognition as well as the sounds the letters make, consider teaching a special lesson about letters that break the rules, as well as blends and digraphs. Whenever possible, let students' names (or names of people in their families) be the catalyst for these lessons.

Name Charts

Cut 13 sheets of poster board vertically in half and write one letter of the alphabet on each half-poster. Hang the small posters on a wall in the classroom or in the hall. Ask students to write their first names on the correct posters. Assign homework for students to write the names of their family members on a piece of paper. The next day, have students transfer names from their papers to the correct posters. Consider creating a separate set of posters for last names, or have students add those to the first set.

Teaching Tip
To assess consonant/sound correspondence, use the form at the end of the Letter Recognition section (page 31).

Extension - To add more names to the name charts, have students write a note to each class in the school, asking for a class roster and explaining what they are doing.

Extension - If students enjoy this experience and want to find more names, have students search through picture books and post character names on the charts or bring in copies of books that suggest different baby names.

Vowel/Sound Correspondence

The goal of phonics instruction is to help students learn and use the alphabetic principle—the understanding that there are systematic and predictable relationships between written letters and spoken sounds. Knowing these relationships helps students recognize familiar words accurately and automatically, and to "decode" new words. Knowing vowel letter/sound relationships is a crucial part of knowing the alphabetic system. Because vowels do not have one single sound, they are not as easy to learn as consonants.

Studying word families supports students as they learn to remember the different vowel sounds. Contrasting word families with vowel sounds helps students discriminate between vowel sounds in their writing (Johnston, 1995). However, for students with phonological difficulties, differentiating between vowel sounds often presents problems that may necessitate more training.

It is generally considered better to teach short vowel sounds first, then teach long vowel sounds. The fact that the long vowels have more than one spelling form creates more difficulty for students. For example, long /a/ is spelled with an *a* in words like *apron* and *April*. It is spelled *a–consonant–e* in words like *ate, bake,* and *face*. It is also spelled *ai* in words like *aid, aim,* and *rain*. It is spelled *ay,* in *day, stay, play,* and *may*. It is also spelled *ei* in *vein, rein,* and *veil*. Finally, it can be spelled *eigh* as in *weigh, eight,* and *freight*. In other words, long /a/ has six different spelling forms. Not only do students have to learn letter sounds, but they also must learn these forms.

This section includes a variety of activities to help students connect letters with their short and long vowel sounds. Activities also address the spelling patterns of various vowels. Many of these activities help students learn to connect the consonant sounds with the vowel sounds to create words. As in the other sections, while some activities are suggested for a particular vowel, most of these activities can be adapted to teach any vowel sound or any consonant sound as well.

Elephants in Elevators: Pretending E Actions

Emphasize the /e/ sound in each direction below. Ask students to listen carefully and pretend to:

- walk like an elephant
- fly like an eagle
- break, scramble, and eat eggs
- look over the edge of a cliff
- ride an elevator
- put on earmuffs
- embroider with a needle and thread
- file fingernails with an emery board
- empty the trash

When you are finished, ask students to identify and say the /e/ sounds.

Memory Matching

Copy the Memory Matching reproducible (page 88) on card stock. Cut apart the cards and store them in a resealable, plastic bag. Place all cards facedown in a grid. Have pairs of students take turns playing the game by turning cards over two at a time and searching for two cards with the same vowel sound. As students turn over the cards, ask them to say the vowel sound (or in the case of two-syllable words, the initial vowel sound) represented by the picture on each card, such as, "Apple, /a/ is the sound of *a* in *apple.*" If desired, copy the answer key (below) and store it with the cards to make the game self-checking.

Answer Key:

bat-fan-apple-rabbit   bed-pen-lemon-bell

fish-bib-pig-milk   dog-sock-box-ostrich

drum-bus-sun-cup

 Suggestions for Vowel Collection Boxes

As suggested in the Consonant Collection Boxes section (page 52), students learn from creating collections of items to represent various vowel sounds. Suggestions follow for creating collections for the vowel sounds. Remind students that pictures of objects or toys may take the place of the real thing. Note that items whose names change the initial letter sound have not been listed. For example, although many states are included in the lists (puzzle pieces can be placed in the collections boxes), Arkansas, for example, is not listed because the initial sounds are not short or long /a/.

A Collection Box Items:
acorn, address book, Alabama, Alaska, alligator, alphabet, apple, ant, ape, ax

E Collection Box Items:
earmuffs, earrings, easel, eel, egg, elephant, elevator, equal sign, eraser, escalator, exclamation point

I Collection Box Items:
ice cream, ice skate, icicle, igloo, iguana, Illinois, inch cubes, inch squares, Indiana, Iowa, index card

O Collection Box Items:
ocean, octopus, Ohio, Oklahoma, okra, olive, ostrich, Othello®, otter, oval, ox

U Collection Box Items:
ukulele, umbrella, umpire, unicorn, unicycle, Utah

Open, Shut Them

Traditional rhymes can be used to help students remember certain letter sounds if the initial sound is repeated and emphasized when the class is chanting the rhyme. "Open, Shut Them" is best used for the long /o/ sound.

Open, shut them. Open, shut them. (Open and shut hands.)
Give a little clap. (Clap hands.)
Open, shut them. Open, shut them. (Open and shut hands.)
Lay them in your lap. (Fold hands in lap.)
Creep them, creep them, creep them, creep them right up to your chin. ("Crawl" up your arms to your chin.)
Open wide your mouth, but do not let them in. (Open mouth and pretend to put hands in, but shut mouth at the last minute.)

Long and Short Vowel Practice

Copy the game board and directions (pages 90-91) on paper and the game cards (pages 91-95) on card stock. Color and cut out the game board and glue it to the inside of a file folder. Glue the directions to the front of the folder. Let students color the pictures on the game cards. Cut out the game cards. Tape each to an index card if you plan to make additional cards or if students find larger cards easier to manipulate. Finally, provide game pieces that can be stored with the game. Let small groups play this game together. Place the cards facedown in a stack. Let the student who draws the first card move to the nearest square that has that sound. Play continues with students drawing cards until one student reaches the finish line. The game can be played to emphasize short vowel sounds, long vowel sounds, or long and short sounds mixed together. Create additional cards if needed by copying one page of cards, covering the illustrations with masking tape, and drawing or cutting out more pictures. (There is a list of picture names at the bottom of each page.)

> **Teaching Tip**
> Draw generic game boards or copy those provided (pages 96-97). Laminate each to a folder. On the path's squares, use a write-on/wipe-away pen to write letters students need to practice. Use magazine pictures or any of the picture cards in this book to make a selection of generic game cards to create games for any phonics skill.

Under the Umbrella

Use *Brown Bear, Brown Bear, What Do You See?* by Bill Martin Jr. (Henry Holt & Company, Inc., 1996) as a model to make a book called *Under the Umbrella*. Photograph students holding umbrellas, or have each student draw a picture of himself under an umbrella. On the first page (for example, under Jordan's picture), write, "Jordan under the umbrella, who do you see?" On the next page (on the back of Jordan's picture), write, "I see Michael looking at me." On the third page (under Michael's picture), write, "Michael under the umbrella, who do you see?" and so on. Read the book in small groups, emphasizing the short /u/ sounds.

Long and Short Vowel Practice

Finish

Sorry! Go back one space.

o   i   a

e

Oops! Lose a turn.

u   i

o

Sorry! Go back one space.

e

a

o   u

Wow! Move ahead two spaces.

i   e   a

Start

Long and Short Vowel Practice

Directions:
1. Shuffle the cards. Place them facedown in a pile.
2. Let the first player draw a card, say the name of the picture, and listen to the first (or only) vowel sound.
3. The first player should move her game piece to the next space that contains the letter that makes that vowel sound.
4. If there are directions on that space, she must follow those directions. It is then the next player's turn.
5. The first person to reach the finish line is the winner.

Picture names are *cat, can, bat, apple, hat, fan, rake, cake, train.*

Long and Short Vowel Practice

Picture names are *gate, nail, tape, net, pen, bed, egg, elephant, bell, eel, queen, key.*

Long and Short Vowel Practice

Picture names are *peas, seal, leaf, fish, lips, milk, chick, igloo, pig, bike, icicle, kite.*

Picture names are *tiger, pie, ice cream, dog, clock, fox, octopus, sock, box, rope, oval, nose* (page 94), and *soap, bow, globe, bug, cup, rug, nuts, sun,*

umbrella, unicorn, unicycle, flute, glue, cube, fruit (page 95).

Generic Game Board

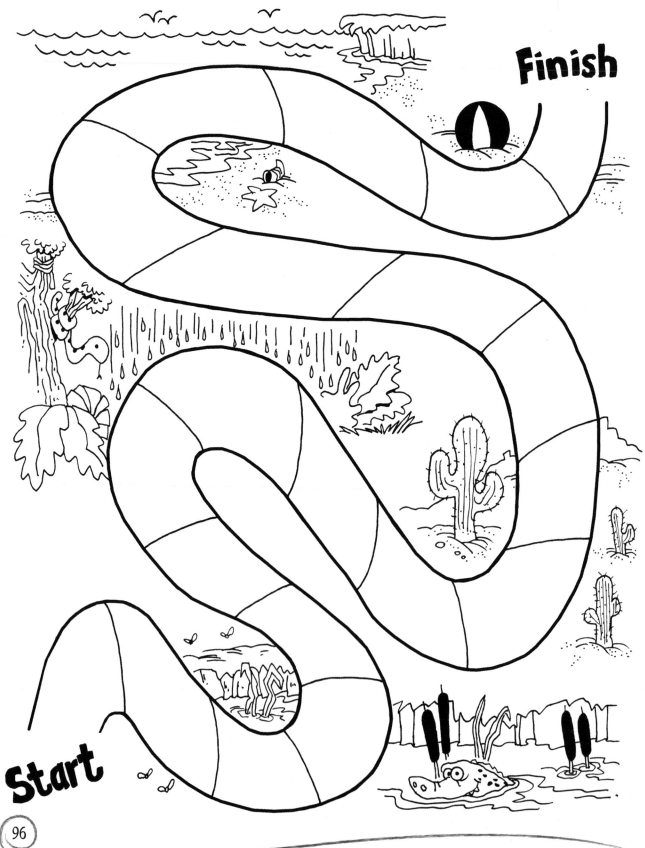

Finish

Start

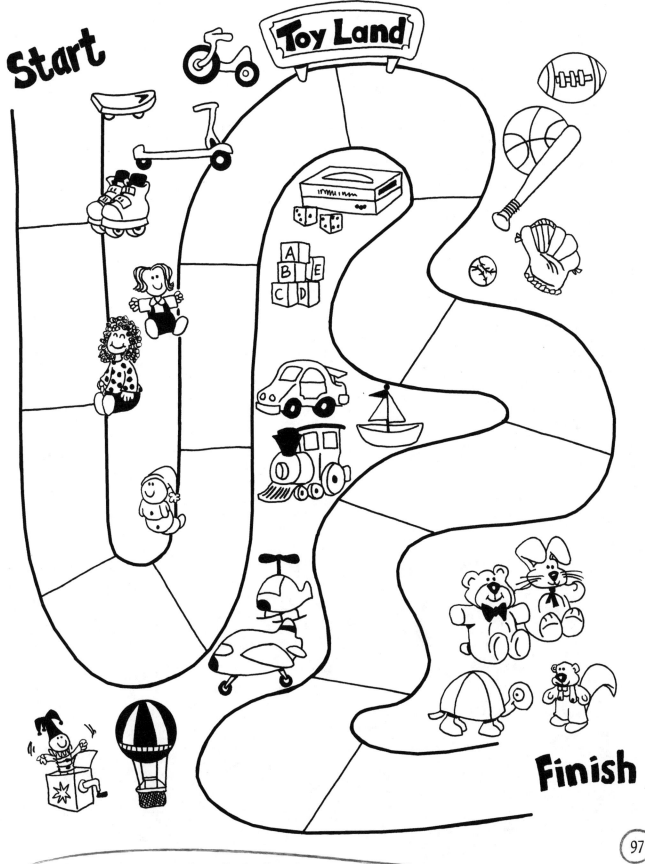

Generic Game Board

Start

Toy Land

Finish

Circus Seal Tricks: Short Vowel Review

Copy the circus seals, directions, answer key, and ball patterns (pages 98-99). Color the patterns. Tape or glue the seals to the inside of a file folder. Tape the directions to the front of the file folder. Let students lightly color the ball patterns, and store them with the answer key in a resealable, plastic bag. Let partners play this game together with one student reading the words on the balls and the other player identifying the vowel sounds and placing the balls by the correct seals.

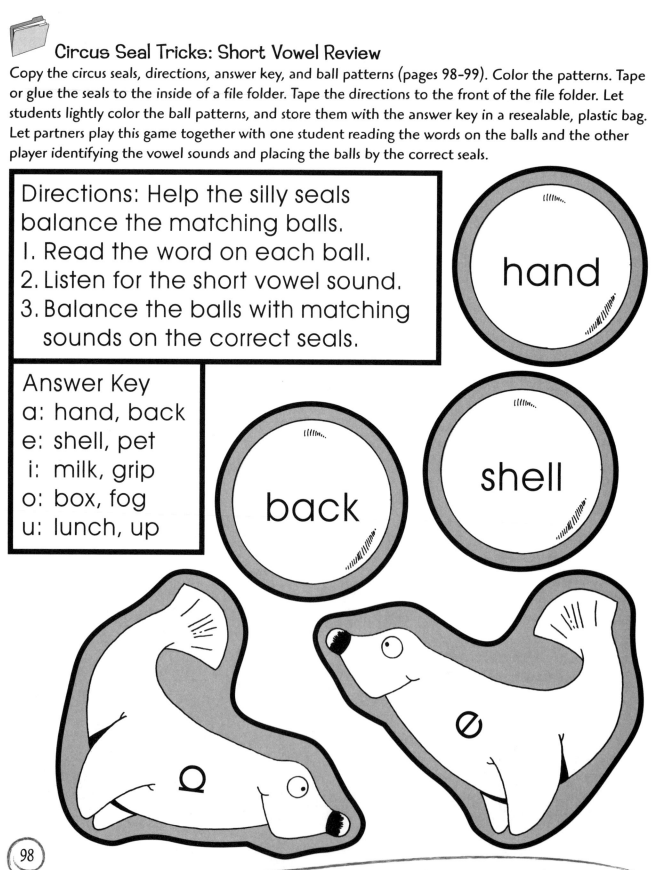

Directions: Help the silly seals balance the matching balls.
1. Read the word on each ball.
2. Listen for the short vowel sound.
3. Balance the balls with matching sounds on the correct seals.

Answer Key
a: hand, back
e: shell, pet
i: milk, grip
o: box, fog
u: lunch, up

hand

back

shell

Circus Seal Tricks: Short Vowel Review

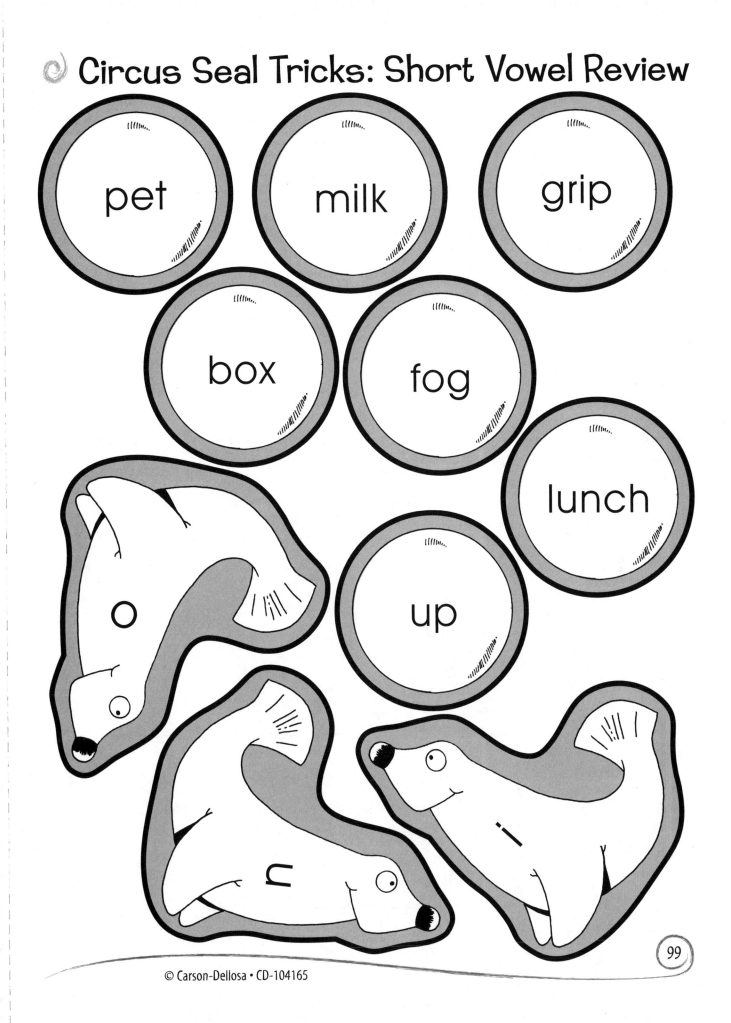

pet

milk

grip

box

fog

lunch

o

up

u

i

99

© Carson-Dellosa • CD-104165

Plant the Flowers: Short and Long Vowel Review

Copy the flowerpots, flowers, directions, and answer key (pages 100-101). Let students color the flowerpots and flowers. Cut out the patterns. Glue the directions to the front of a file folder and the flowerpots to the inside of the folder. Store the answer key and flowers in a resealable, plastic bag. Let partners play this game together with one student reading the word on each flower and the other student identifying the vowel sound and placing the flower in the correct flowerpot. Use the blank flower patterns to make additional words for students to match.

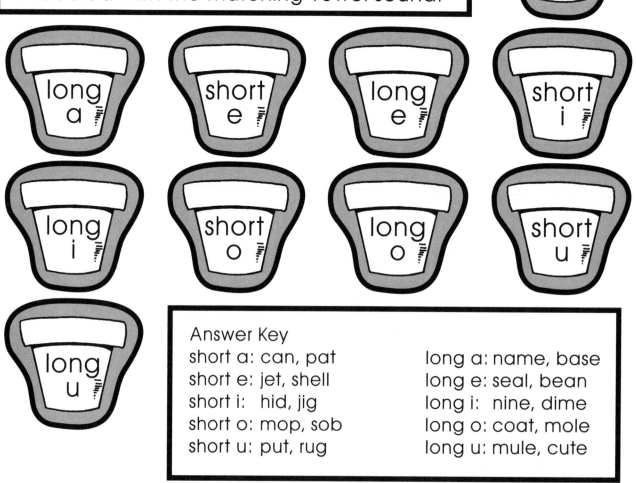

Directions: Plant the flowers in the right pots.
1. Read the word on each flower.
2. Listen for the vowel sound.
3. Place each flower in the pot that is labeled with the matching vowel sound.

short a

long a   short e   long e   short i

long i   short o   long o   short u

long u

Answer Key

short a: can, pat   long a: name, base
short e: jet, shell   long e: seal, bean
short i: hid, jig   long i: nine, dime
short o: mop, sob   long o: coat, mole
short u: put, rug   long u: mule, cute

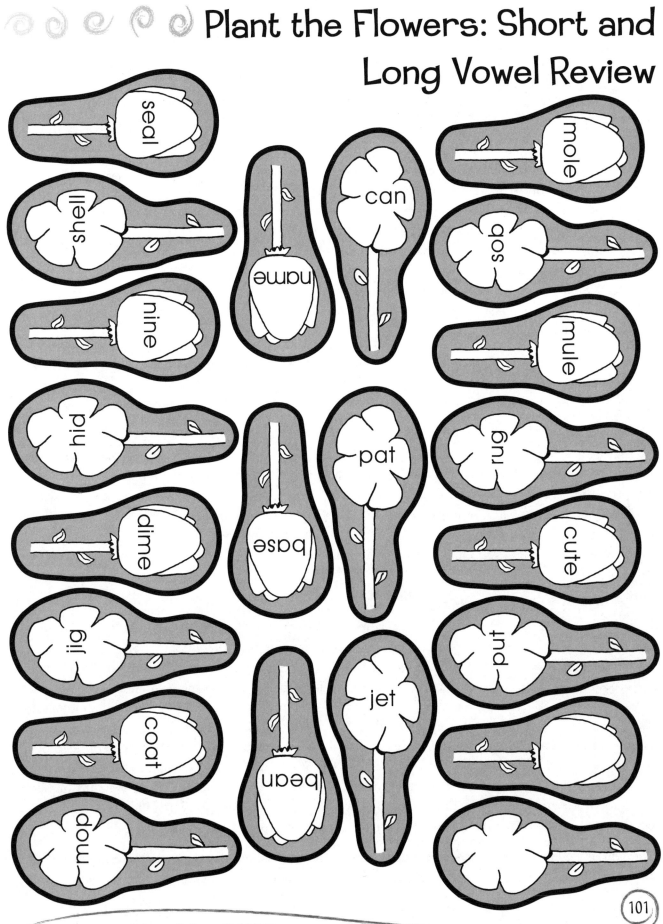

Teacher's Helper: Tasting Experiences for Remembering Vowel Sounds

As with consonant sounds, students who have trouble remembering vowel sounds benefit from connecting a specific word to each letter. Active experiences like eating help students remember a word to associate with a beginning sound. Below are several suggestions of foods to represent each vowel. Use foods with familiar brand names to expand the activity.

A - apples, applesauce, avocado, acorn squash, asparagus
E - eggs, eggplant, egg rolls, escarole, endive, elephant ears
I - ice cream bars, ice cream sandwiches, ice cubes
O - okra, olives, omelets, oatmeal, oatmeal cookies
U - upside-down cake, Ugli fruit®

Extension – Using pictures from seed catalogs, grocery circulars, and coupons, have students create a food poster for each letter of the alphabet.

> **Teaching Tip**
> When planning a food activity, be sure to get parental permission and check for allergies and religious or other preferences.

Magic E

On index cards, write *pan, pane, rat, rate, bit, bite, rip, ripe, not, note, ton, tone, tub, tube, cub, cube.* Write each short-vowel word on the front, and its long-vowel counterpart on the back. Tell students to watch for the magic "e." Wave a "magic wand" and say, "It is so special that it does not need to say its name but can cast a spell on other vowels so that they say their own names." Then, share an index card with the short vowel sound, wave the wand, flip over the card, and show the long vowel word. Have students say the words as you show them the index cards.

Vowel Sound Dominoes

Reproduce multiple copies of pages 103–117. There are seven different vowel sound games for children to play: short /a/ and short /e/, long /a/ and long /e/, long /o/ and long /i/, long /a/ and short /a/, long /e/ and short /e/, long /o/ and short /o/, and long /i/ and short /i/. Use a glue stick to attach the cards to card stock or reproduce them directly on card stock. Laminate the cards for durability, then separate the dominoes into seven different resealable bags. (Put cards from pages 103–104 into one bag, cards from 105–106 into another bag, and so on.) Teach children to play this type of dominoes by placing all cards in one set facedown. The first player should choose one card and place it faceup in the middle of the table. The second player should then choose a card and match it to the correct end of the first domino. Play continues until all dominoes have been played. (There is a list of the picture names with matching vowel sounds. Review picture names with students to avoid confusion. Blank domino templates can be found on page 117. Use the blank templates to create additional dominoes from clip art or pictures cut from magazines.)

Extension – If students can identify long vowel sounds, use all cards at once. Let each player draw five cards and match the ends. If a player cannot make a play, he must draw another card and lose his turn.

Vowel Sound Dominoes

Picture names are:
- rabbit-pen
- bag-bed
- cap-elephant
- ant-head
- can-net

Vowel Sound Dominoes

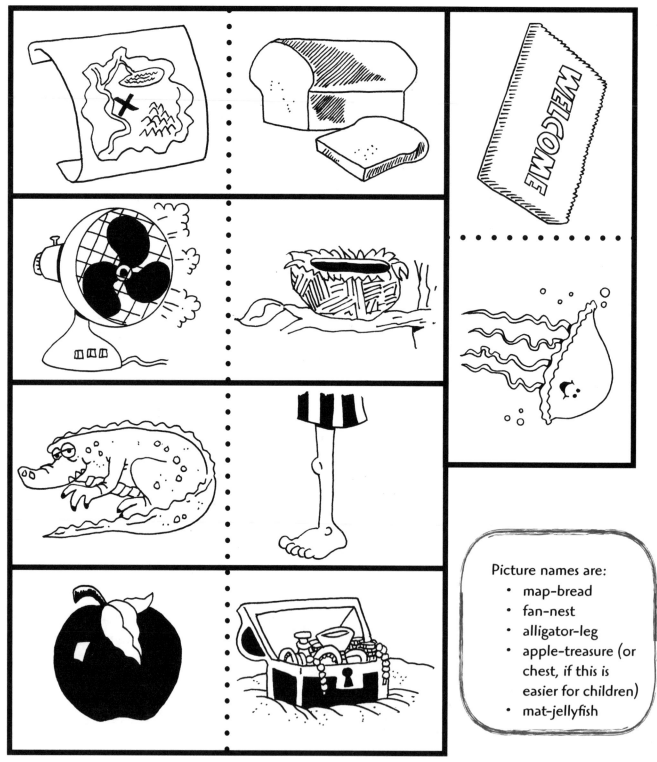

Picture names are:
- map–bread
- fan–nest
- alligator–leg
- apple–treasure (or chest, if this is easier for children)
- mat–jellyfish

Vowel Sound Dominoes

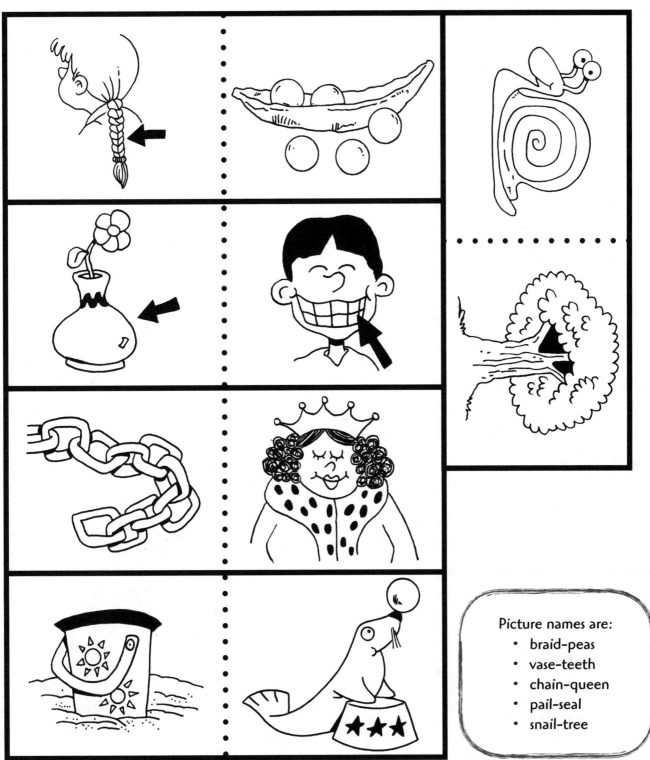

Picture names are:
- braid-peas
- vase-teeth
- chain-queen
- pail-seal
- snail-tree

Vowel Sound Dominoes

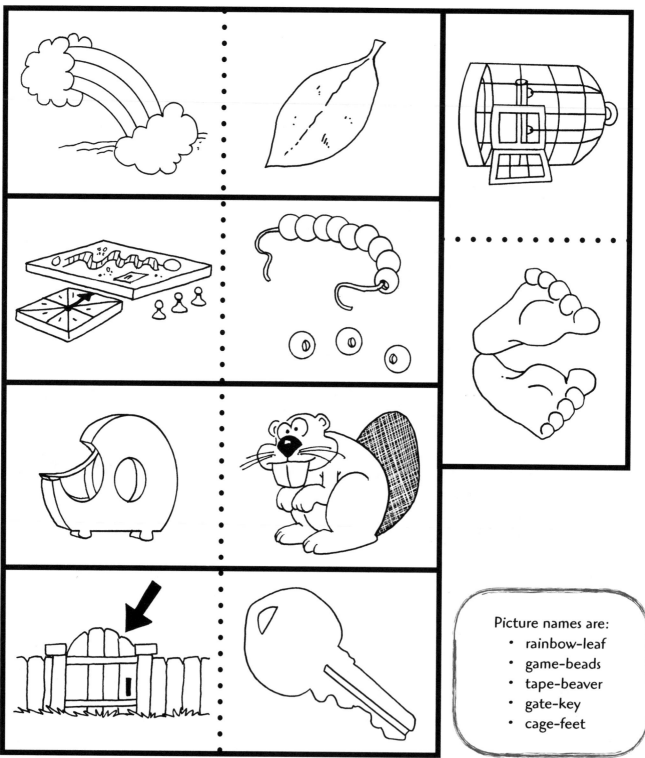

Picture names are:
- rainbow-leaf
- game-beads
- tape-beaver
- gate-key
- cage-feet

Picture names are:
- bowl–bike
- soap–nine
- yo-yo–fire
- rose–kite
- toe–dice

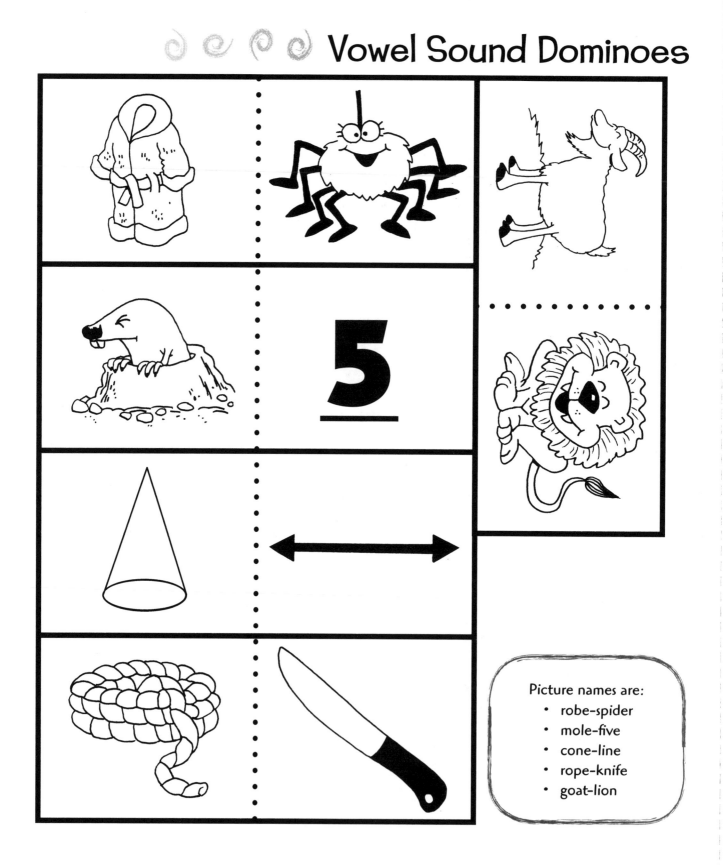

Picture names are:
- robe-spider
- mole-five
- cone-line
- rope-knife
- goat-lion

Vowel Sound Dominoes

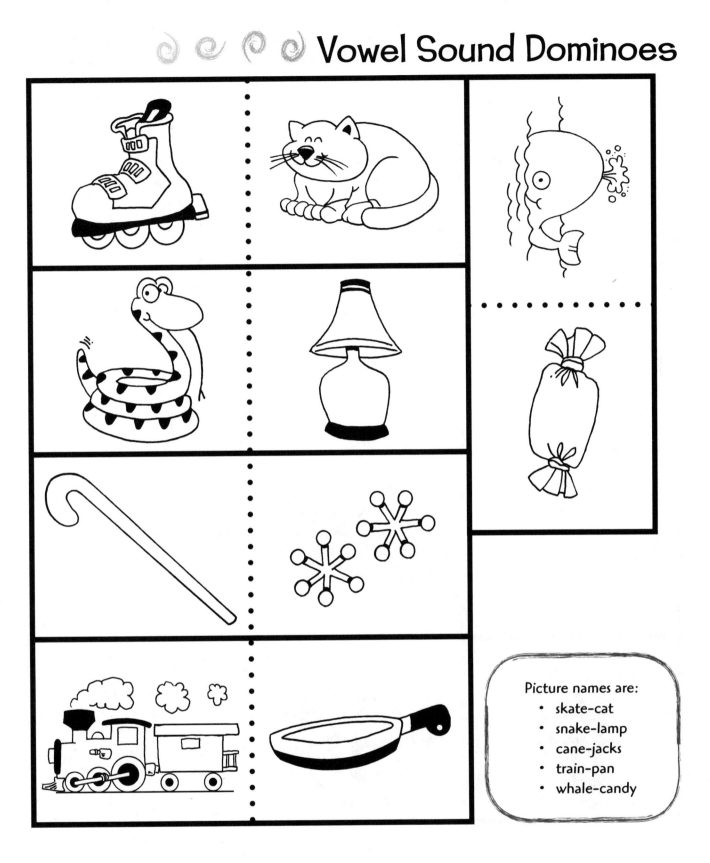

Picture names are:
- skate-cat
- snake-lamp
- cane-jacks
- train-pan
- whale-candy

Vowel Sound Dominoes

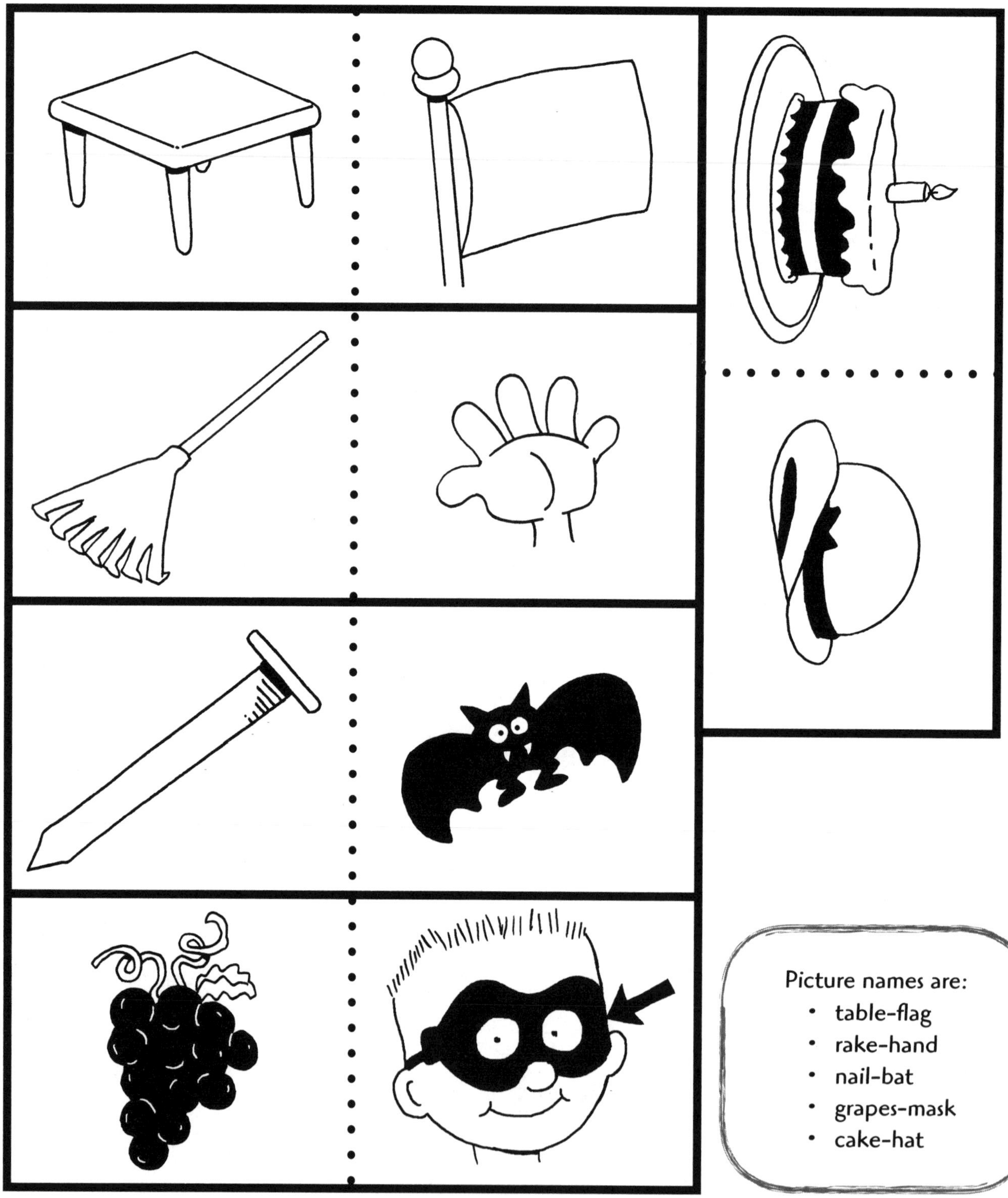

Picture names are:
- table-flag
- rake-hand
- nail-bat
- grapes-mask
- cake-hat

110

Picture names are:
- cheese-feather
- knee-well
- peach-bench
- bee-desk
- sheep-bell

3 | **10**

Picture names are:
- three-ten
- cheek-dress
- wheel-tent
- geese-seven
- heel-neck

7

Vowel Sound Dominoes

Picture names are:
- nose-frog
- goat-doll
- stove-knot
- hose-clock
- bow-mop

Vowel Sound Dominoes

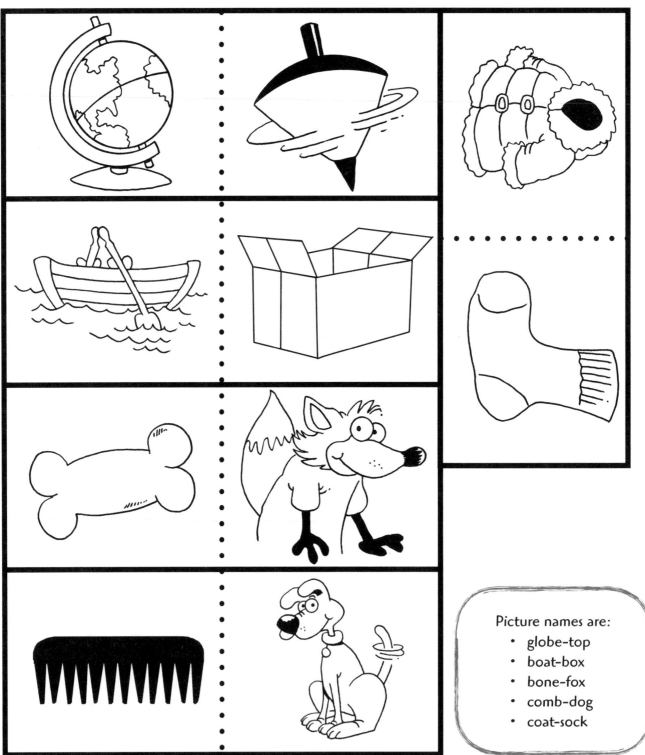

Picture names are:
- globe-top
- boat-box
- bone-fox
- comb-dog
- coat-sock

Vowel Sound Dominoes

Picture names are:
- vine-chick
- fly-milk
- slide-lips
- hive-fist
- pie-six

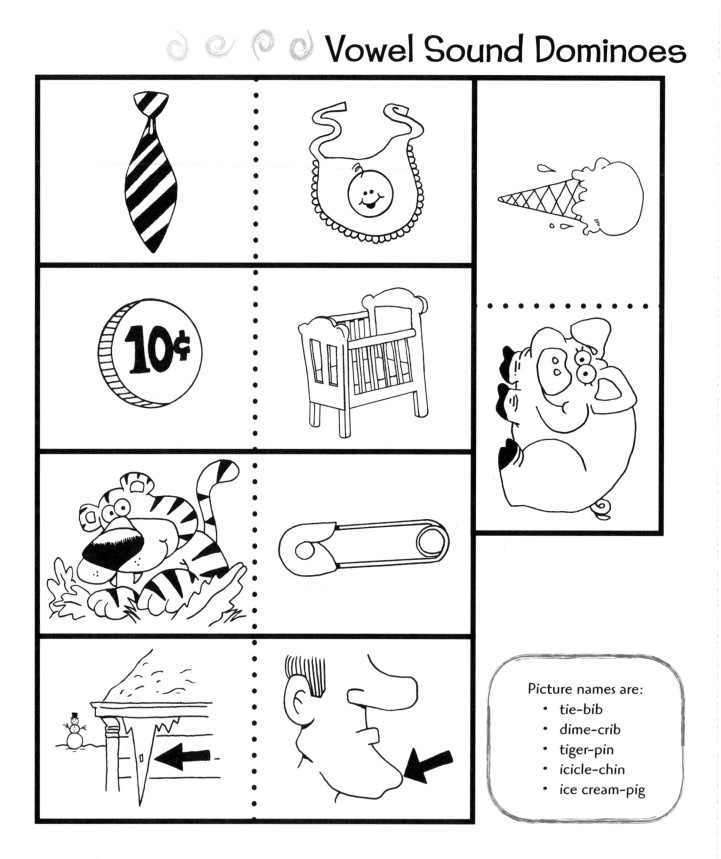

Picture names are:
- tie-bib
- dime-crib
- tiger-pin
- icicle-chin
- ice cream-pig

Vowel Sound Dominoes

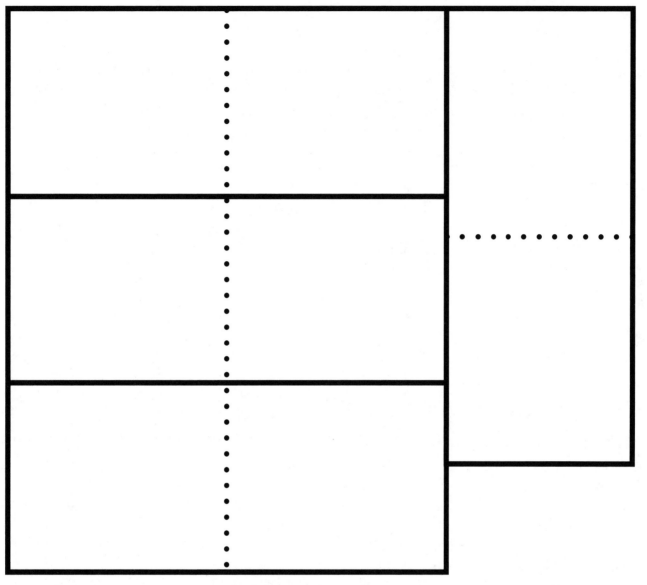

Picture Names with Matching Vowel Sounds

Short /a/: alligator, ant, apple, bag, bat, can, candy, cap, cat, fan, flag, hand, hat, jacks, lamp, map, mask, mat, pan, rabbit

Long /a/: braid, cage, cake, cane, chain, game, gate, grapes, nail, pail, rainbow, rake, skate, snail, snake, table, tape, train, vase, whale

Short /e/: bed, bell, bench, bread, desk, dress, elephant, feather, head, jellyfish, leg, neck, nest, net, pen, seven, ten, tent, treasure (or chest), well

Long /e/: beads, beaver, bee, cheek, cheese, feet, geese, heel, key, knee, leaf, peach, peas, queen, seal, sheep, teeth, three, tree, wheel

Short /i/: bib, chick, chin, crib, fist, lips, milk, pig, pin, six

Long /i/: bike, dice, dime, fire, five, fly, hive, ice cream, icicle, kite, knife, line, lion, nine, pie, slide, spider, tie, tiger, vine

Short /o/: box, clock, dog, doll, fox, frog, knot, mop, sock, top

Long /o/: boat, bone, bow, bowl, coat, comb, cone, globe, goat, hose, mole, nose, robe, rope, rose, soap, stove, toe, yo-yo

Long Vowels - Short Vowels

Copy the Long Vowels – Short Vowels pictures (pages 119-121) onto card stock, laminate them, and cut them apart. Copy the directions (below) on colorful paper and glue them to the front of a file folder. Copy the answer key and store it with the pictures. Label the left inside panel of the folder "Long Vowels" and the right inside panel "Short Vowels." Have pairs or individuals sort the pictures by placing them on either the left or right side of the folder. Remind them to listen for the first vowel sound in each picture name.

Directions: Place the pictures with short vowels under the words Short Vowels. Place the pictures with long vowels under the words Long Vowels.

Answer Key
short /a/: apple, alligator, mask, ant, pan
long /a/: cake, snake, grapes, nail, skate
short /e/: bell, egg, net, leg, nest
long /e/: knee, seal, tree, leaf, wheel
short /i/: pig, six, crib, milk, bib
long /i/: dice, bike, kite, tiger, tie
short /o/: frog, fox, dog, box, mop
long /o/: nose, globe, rose, boat, toe
short /u/: bus, sun, umbrella, truck
long /u/: fruit, flute, unicycle, unicorn

Apples and Bananas

Students enjoy singing the traditional song "Apples and Bananas." It is a clever way to substitute phonemes in words to make a silly song. A recorded version is available from Raffi's CD *One Light, One Sun* (Rounder, 1996). Teach the lyrics below and then have students substitute the different long vowel sounds as they sing.

I like to eat, eat, eat apples and bananas
I like to eat, eat, eat apples and bananas

I like to ate, ate, ate ay-ples and ba-nay-nays
I like to ate, ate, ate ay-ples and ba-nay-nays

I like to eat, eat, eat ee-ples and bee-nee-nees
I like to eat, eat, eat ee-ples and bee-nee-nees

I like to ite, ite, ite i-ples and by-ny-nys
I like to ite, ite, ite i-ples and by-ny-nys

I like to ote, ote, ote oh-ples and bo-no-nos
I like to ote, ote, ote oh-ples and bo-no-nos

I like to oot, oot, oot oo-ples and boo-noo-noos
I like to oot, oot, oot oo-ples and boo-noo-noos

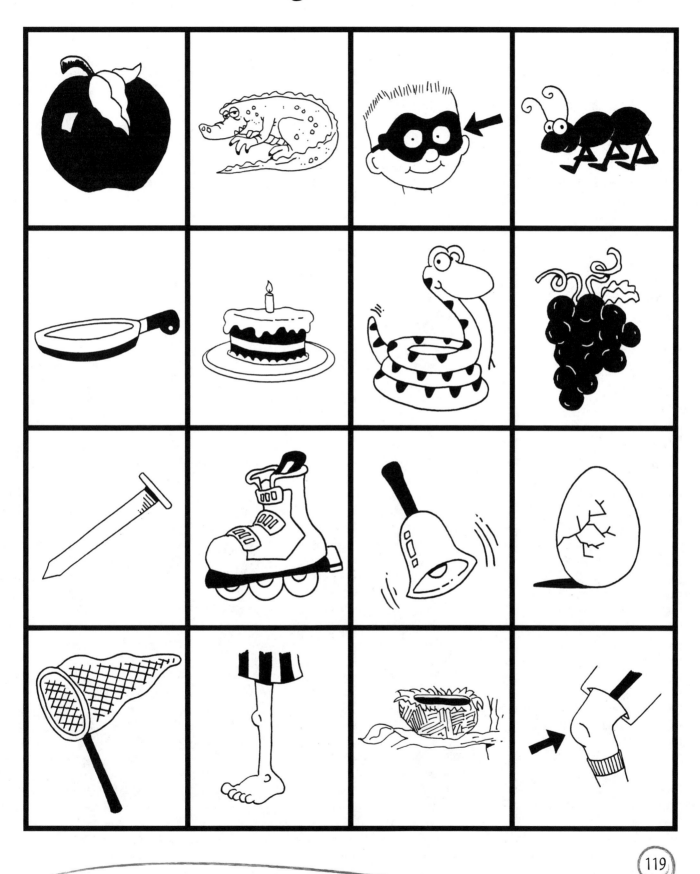

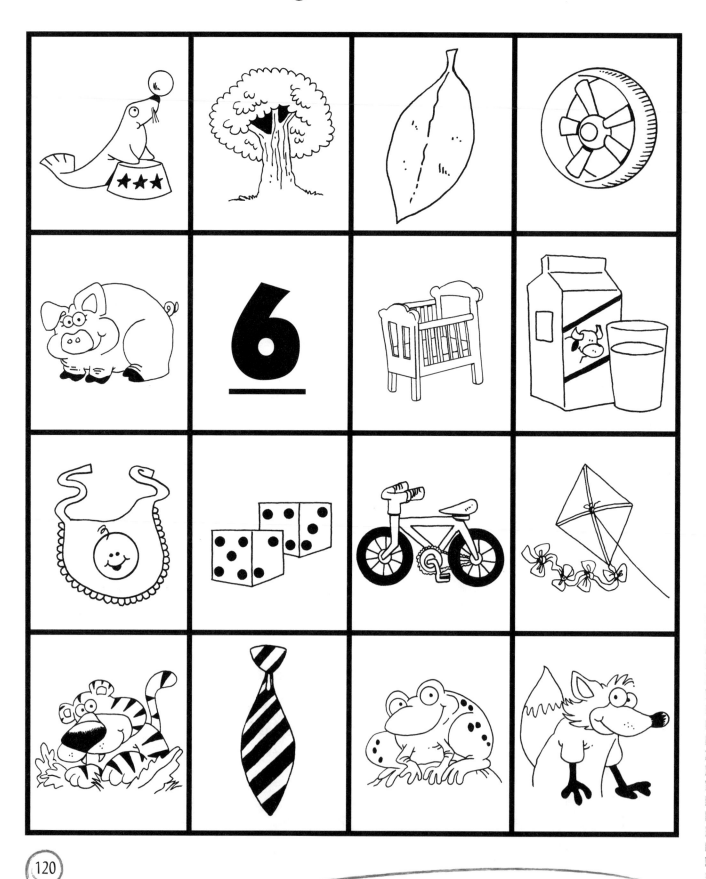

Long Vowels – Short Vowels

Name That Word

Copy the clues (pages 122–124) on card stock and cut them apart. Attach the cards together by punching a hole in the corner of each and threading them on a ring. During short periods of time between lessons, give clues that must be answered with words that have the various vowel sounds. Either announce the required vowel sound in advance or, after giving the questions, ask students to identify the common vowel sound used.

Name a fruit. Vowel sound: (short /a/) Answer: apple	Name a piece of sports equipment. Vowel sound: (short /a/) Answer: bat	Name the school subject that relates to numbers. Vowel sound: (short /a/) Answer: math
Name the thing you put on a horse before you ride it. Vowel sound: (short /a/) Answer: saddle	Name the place where most people keep their money. Vowel sound: (short /a/) Answer: bank	Name something you eat at a birthday party. Vowel sound: (long /a/) Answer: cake
Name a reptile that has no legs. Vowel sound: (long /a/) Answer: snake	Name a fruit. Vowel sound: (long /a/) Answer: grape	Name where you run in the game of softball. Vowel sound: (long /a/) Answer: base
Name something we like to play during recess. Vowel sound: (long /a/) Answer: games	Name something to eat for breakfast. Vowel sound: (short /e/) Answer: eggs	Name a number. Vowel sound: (short /e/) Answer: seven or ten
		Name something to write with. Vowel sound: (short /e/) Answer: pen or pencil

Name the nickname for an animal doctor. Vowel sound: (short /e/) Answer: vet or veterinarian	**Name a fast airplane.** Vowel sound: (short /e/) Answer: jet	**Name an insect that stings.** Vowel sound: (long /e/) Answer: bee
Name the part of your leg that bends. Vowel sound: (long /e/) Answer: knee	**Name a farm animal.** Vowel sound: (long /e/) Answer: sheep	**Name a large plant.** Vowel sound: (long /e/) Answer: tree
Name what you do at night. Vowel sound: (long /e/) Answer: sleep or dream	**Name something that has six legs.** Vowel sound: (short /i/) Answer: insect	**Name what you do when you pick up something.** Vowel sound: (short /i/) Answer: lift
Name a farm animal. Vowel sound: (short /i/) Answer: pig	**Name something you do in a pool.** Vowel sound: (short /i/) Answer: swim	**Name what you should do when you come to your chair.** Vowel sound: (short /i/) Answer: sit
Name what an adult does in a car. Vowel sound: (long /i/) Answer: drive	**Name small rodents.** Vowel sound: (long /i/) Answer: mice	**Name a color.** Vowel sound: (long /i/) Answer: white
Name what you call water after it freezes. Vowel sound: (long /i/) Answer: ice	**Name what you are looking for when you look at a clock.** Vowel sound: (long /i/) Answer: time	**Name a bird that cannot fly.** Vowel sound: (short /o/) Answer: ostrich

123

Name a word that means many or much. Vowel sound: (short /o/) Answer: lots	**Name an ocean animal that has eight legs.** Vowel sound: (short /o/) Answer: octopus	**Name a small body of water.** Vowel sound: (short /o/) Answer: pond
Name the word on the red sign you see at street corners. Vowel sound: (short /o/) Answer: stop	**Name a short word for what you use to talk to people who are far away.** Vowel sound: (long /o/) Answer: phone	**Name what you call a round map of the world.** Vowel sound: (long /o/) Answer: globe
Name the part of the body that can smell things. Vowel sound: (long /o/) Answer: nose	**Name a place to drive a car.** Vowel sound: (long /o/) Answer: road	**Name something that protects you when it rains.** Vowel sound: (short /u/) Answer: umbrella
Name something you chew but do not swallow. Vowel sound: (short /u/) Answer: gum	**Name something grown-ups pour coffee into.** Vowel sound: (short /u/) Answer: cup or mug	**Name something you do when you play soccer.** Vowel sound: (short /u/) Answer: run
Name the vehicle some students ride to school. Vowel sound: (short /u/) Answer: bus	**Name a month.** Vowel sound: (long /u/) Answer: June or July	**Name the shape of a die.** Vowel sound: (long /u/) Answer: cube
Name a color. Vowel sound: (long /u/) Answer: blue	**Name a liquid you use to stick things together.** Vowel sound: (long /u/) Answer: glue	**Name another word for song.** Vowel sound: (long /u/) Answer: tune

Vowel Sounds Relay

Complete this activity outside where students can make noise and where you can draw on the sidewalk. On separate cards, draw the symbols and letters for each of the short and long vowel sounds. Make two sets of cards. Assign the whole class to two teams. Have the teams line up facing each other. Ask the first student from each team to stand in front of you. Call out a word and have students pull out the card with the vowel sound they think is in that word. On your signal, have each student hold up his guess as to what the vowel sound is. If a student is correct and is the first to hold up his card, use sidewalk chalk to draw a tally mark on the ground in front of his team. Continue until each student has had a turn.

Extension – Play this game on several different days, one time for each vowel sound. At the end of each game, celebrate with a reward containing that vowel sound, such as eating apples and bananas for snack (short /a/), playing another game (long /a/), getting extra free time (short or long /e/), etc. (Be sure to get families' permission and check for food allergies and religious or other preferences before completing any food activity.)

Pease Porridge Hot

To reinforce the difference in long /o/ and short /o/ sounds, chant the following traditional poem and ask students to identify the words that have the long /o/ sound and those that have the short /o/ sound.

Pease porridge hot.
Pease porridge cold.
Pease porridge in the pot.
Nine days old.

Some like it hot.
Some like it cold.
Some like it in the pot.
Nine days old.

Assessment of Vowel/Sound Correspondence

For assessment of Awareness of Vowel/Sound Correspondence, use the form at the end of the Letter Recognition section (page 31). Simply mark out the consonants and assess for only the vowels.

Teaching Tip

Use the Vowel Sounds Relay activity to review single or initial vowel sounds in sight words, adjectives, and verbs that are hard to draw. Examples include *am, an, and, at, can, have, name, say, may, play, way, every, get, let, tell, wet, be, he, me, she, the, did, this, which, wish, with, by, my, time, try, why, got, long, not, off, stop, know, no, over, own, so, us, under, up, choose,* and *use.* Be sure to make a list beforehand to avoid calling out a word that has more than one vowel sound.

Initial and Final Sounds of Words

After students learn the relationships between letters and the sounds associated with them, typically the next step in helping students learn to read is to begin teaching the easier types of phonological awareness. Phoneme manipulation, such as identifying initial sounds in words, is one of these easier types. After students develop the ability to identify initial sounds in words, instruction in identifying final and medial sounds in words can begin. As students master those skills, the more advanced types of phonemic awareness, such as segmenting, blending, deletion/addition, and substitution can be introduced.

Alliterative Name Sentences

Begin each morning meeting with three or four sentences about students in the classroom. In each sentence, include at least one other word that begins with the same letter sound as the initial sound of each student's name. The sentences can be silly or factual. Some examples might be:

Alice, I heard you ate apples and asparagus for dinner last night.

Felicia, you look fantastic.

Mitchell, did you move on Monday morning?

Silly Sentences

Say a "silly sentence," such as, "Marty Miller moved many messy monkeys on Monday." Discuss how the sentence is silly. Is it silly to think of a monkey as being messy? How do you move a monkey? Help the students notice that many of the words began with the same letter. Have them identify the /m/. Then, challenge students to think of silly sentences for other initial letter sounds.

• • Going Places

Ask each student to think of a place that he wants to go. Then, have volunteers tell three things to take along that have the same beginning sound as the place they want to go. For example, a student might say, "I'm going to the beach and I'm taking a ball, a bottle, and a baboon." Students' responses do not have to make sense; they only need to have matching sounds.

• • What's the End?

Display several objects on a table. Ask a student to select an object and say its name. Then, have his classmates say words that have the same ending sound. For example, if the student selects a bell, his classmates should respond with words like *will, meal, sell,* etc. Remind students that they are focusing on sounds, not spellings.

Extension – Vary the game by playing "What's the Beginning?" as you focus on initial sounds, or "What's the Middle?" by focusing on medial sounds.

• • Whisper the Magic Sound

Ask students to stand in a circle. Select one student to be the "listener." Select one sound to be the "magic sound" and tell the "listener" to listen for that sound. Designate the other students to be "whisperers." Ask each "whisperer" to select a letter card and whisper the sounds of their letters—all at the same time. The "listener" should slowly walk around the circle trying to distinguish the "magic sound." When the "listener" hears the sound, he should identify the student who was whispering it. The "whisperer" with the correct sound becomes the next "listener." The "whisperers" can continue to pronounce the same sound or trade sounds with each other while this new "listener" listens for the next sound. Note that whispering will make some sounds, such as /b/ and /p/, difficult to distinguish.

• Treasure Hunt

Tell the students that treasure is hidden in the room. Give each student an index card with a letter written on it. Challenge each student to find her "treasure." The treasure can be any object in the classroom that begins with that letter sound. After students find their treasures, ask them to come back to the meeting area. Then, each student, in turn, should report his letter and show the object to the whole group.

Pajama Party Day

Have a pajama party day where students wear pajamas to school and plan activities that begin with the /p/ sound, such as making peanut butter, creating paper-bag puppets, putting on a puppet show, planting petunias, making paper planes, chanting the tongue twister "Peter Piper Picked a Peck of Pickled Peppers," eating Popsicles® and making Popsicle® stick puzzles, popping popcorn, reading the traditional story of *The Three Little Pigs* as well as the popular spin-off *The True Story of the Three Little Pigs* by Jon Scieszka (Puffin, 1996), making pizzas for lunch, and so on. (Before completing any food activity, be sure to get families' permission and check for food allergies and religious or other preferences.)

Extension - Change the focus of this activity to suit any letter by changing the article of clothing. For example, focus on the letter *h* by having Hat Day, or plan to make necklaces in class for the letter *n*.

Sorting Silly Socks

Proclaim a *Silly Socks* day. Ask students to wear silly socks (socks that do not match) to school and allow them to take off their shoes for the duration of the school day, except for the times when they leave the classroom. Provide a pile of socks in different sizes, colors, patterns, etc., for students to sort. During the sorting activity, emphasize the /s/ sound when talking about sorting silly socks.

Extension - Emphasize the letter *m* instead by changing the sock sorting activity to mitten matching.

Hot and Cold

Continue with the clothing theme while focusing on the letters *h* and *c*. First, have students look at a faucet with labeled handles and tell how they know which handle to turn in order to make the water hotter or colder. Provide clothing that is suitable for hot and cold weather, such as a T-shirt, a swimsuit, shorts, mittens, a scarf, etc. Label a large box with an *H* and another with a *C*. Have students sort the clothing into the appropriate boxes.

Extension - The clothing and temperature activities will also work with warm and cool, wet and dry, rainy or sunny, etc.

Reading *Have You Seen My Cat?*

Read *Have You Seen My Cat?* by Eric Carle (Little Simon, 1996). The repetition of the question, "Have you seen my cat?" makes it easy to focus on the initial sounds in these words. Choose one word for each reading and focus on that letter sound: /h/, /y/, /s/, /m/, or /k/.

Clara Caterpillar: Connecting Literature with Initial /k/

Read *Clara Caterpillar* by Pamela Duncan Edwards (HarperCollins, 2001). Although the author does not keep the /k/ sound pure because she includes blends and digraphs that begin with *c*, she uses quite a bit of alliteration in telling this story. Other butterflies make fun of Clara because she is such a plain butterfly, but her cream color allows her to hide from enemies and save other fancier-looking butterflies. After reading the book, ask students to create butterflies for a bulletin board and give all of the butterflies names that begin with *c*.

Extension – To add a science twist to the lesson, cover a bulletin board with several different sheets of wrapping paper, and challenge students to decorate their butterflies so that they blend in with the paper. Teach students the word *camouflage*, emphasizing the /k/ sound.

Elmer: Connecting Literature with Short /e/ in the Initial Position

Read the book *Elmer* by David McKee (HarperCollins, 1989), emphasizing the short /e/ sound throughout the book. Sketch an elephant on a large piece of chart paper. Cut different colors of tissue paper into 1" squares. Allow students to work in small groups to glue tissue paper onto the elephant to create an Elmer for the classroom. After the glue has dried, make a name tag for the elephant, asking students to read "Elmer the Elephant" on the tag as they emphasize the initial short /e/ sound.

Extension – To further emphasize the short /e/ sound, have students look through catalogs and clip art to locate pictures of objects that begin with this sound. Then, cut out the pictures, and glue them around the elephant's edges.

Extension – Introduce the /w/ sound using the sequel *Elmer and Wilbur* by David McKee (HarperCollins 2004).

129

Finny Finds Friends in the Forest: Finding Fs

Read *Finny Finds Friends in the Forest* by Tini Sisters and Erin Marie Mauterer (Atori Publishing, 2002). These authors focus on the letter *f*. The text is both alliterative and Dr. Seuss-like in rhythm and rhyme. After the initial read-aloud, reread the book and let volunteers use highlighting tape to identify all words that begin with *f*.

The Letters Are Lost!: Searching for Lost Letters

Locate a set of small alphabet blocks. Hide them around the classroom. Read *The Letters Are Lost* by Lisa Campbell Ernst (Puffin, 1999). Explain that just like in the story, letters are lost in the classroom. Give each student an index card with one letter written on it. Challenge him to find that block, bring it to you, and say the sound associated with that letter.

The Piggy in the Puddle: Connecting Literature with the Initial /p/ sound

Read the rhyming book *The Piggy in the Puddle* by Charlotte Pomerantz (Aladdin, 1989). This is the story of a little pig that plays in a mud puddle and will not come out when her family asks her to. Ask each student to draw, color, and cut out a little pig. Make a batch of instant pudding and let each student scoop the pudding on an individual paper plate and trace her finger in it to make the letter *p*. Finally, let each student place her pig in the "mud."

Extension – Two other books that effectively combine stories about animals with rhyming words are *Pigs in the Mud in the Middle of the Rud* by Lynn Plourde (Scholastic, 1997) and *Sheep in a Jeep* by Nancy E. Shaw (Houghton Mifflin, 1997).

The Quilt: Making a Quilt with the Initial /q/ Sound

Read *The Quilt* by Ann Jonas (Greenwillow, 1984). Distribute squares of various colors of construction paper and ask students to use markers to write uppercase and lowercase *Q*s on their papers. When finished, post the squares on a wall or bulletin board to look like a quilt.

Roll Over! A Counting Song: Connecting Initial /r/ with Actions

Read *Roll Over! A Counting Song* by Merle Peek (Clarion Books, 1999). Students will quickly join in reading this familiar poem. Emphasize the /r/ sound at the beginning of the word *roll* and at the end of the word *over*. If there is sufficient room in the class, read the book aloud and let students lie down on the floor and roll over each time they hear the phrase *roll over*.

Silly Sally: Connecting Initial /s/ with Familiar Occurrences

Read *Silly Sally* by Audrey Wood (Harcourt, 1992), a tale with rhyming text that describes a silly woman and the people she meets on her way into town. After reading the story, let students brainstorm other alliterative names that begin with the /s/ sound, such as Simple Simon, Silent Sidney, etc.

Tina, The Teeny Tiny Terrier: Where did all of these initial /t/ sounds come from?

Read *Tina, The Teeny Tiny Terrier* by Leslie Chase (LC2 Books, 2001), a great story about a girl who lives in New York City with her dog. Focus on the /t/ alliteration in the title and note other /t/ words in the book and illustrations, such as *tight, toys, toothbrush,* etc. On the cover, note that Tina is traveling in a tote bag, and later in a taxi. Challenge students to make up stories about Tina's adventures using as many /t/ words as possible.

Watch William Walk: Going Walking, Walking, Walking with initial /w/

Read *Watch William Walk* by Ann Jonas (Greenwillow, 1997), a simple story about two children, William and Wilma, who go for a walk on the beach with Wally, a dog, and Wanda, a duck. The focus is on alliteration more than plot. As you read the book aloud, encourage students to listen for /w/ words and act out the story.

Yummers!: Tasting the Initial /y/ Sound

Read *Yummers!* by James Marshall (Houghton Mifflin, 1986), a story of two friends who go on a long walk to lose weight but end up stopping every few minutes for snacks. The recipe for Yummers is at the end of the book. Having the memory of the title of a book and a specific cooking experience helps students remember the /y/ sound.

Teacher's Helper: Picture Books to Emphasize Initial Sounds

Teachers should not choose books for class read-alouds just because they feature a certain letter or letter sound. However, it is appropriate to use many quality picture books with your students. Including a brief phonics lesson about the connection between the initial letter of the title and the sound associated with it will extend students' learning.

A - *Abuela* by Arthur Dorros (Puffin, 1997)

B - *Bats* by Gail Gibbons (Holiday House, 2000)

C - *Cat's Colors* by Jane Cabrera (Puffin, 2000)

D - *Daydreamers* by Tom Feelings and Eloise Greenfield (Puffin, 1993)

E - *Emily* by Michael Bedard (Doubleday, 1992)

F - *Fortunately* by Remy Charlip (Aladdin, 1993)

G - *Galimoto* by Karen Lynn Williams (HarperTrophy, 1991)

H - *Harbor* by Donald Crews (HarperTrophy, 1987)

I - *Imogene's Antlers* by David Small (Dragonfly Books, 1988)

J - *Jamberry* by Bruce Degen (HarperCollins, 1983)

K - *Keepers* by Jeri Hanel Watts (Lee & Low Books, 2000)

L - *Lost!* by David McPhail (Little, Brown, 1993)

M - *Max* by Bob Graham (Candlewick, 2002)

N - *Noisy Nora* by Rosemary Wells (Viking Books, 1999)

O - *Olivia* by Ian Falconer (Atheneum, 2000)

P - *Parade* by Donald Crews (HarperTrophy, 1986)

Q - *The Quilt* by Ann Jonas (Greenwillow, 1984)

R - *Rain* by Robert Kalan (HarperTrophy, 1991)

S - *Silly Sally* by Audrey Wood (Harcourt, 1992)

T - *Tigress* by Helen Cowcher (Farrar, Straus and Giroux, 1993)

U - *The Ugly Duckling* by Hans Christian Andersen (HarperCollins, 1999)

V - *Victor Vito and Freddie Vasco* by Laurie Berkner (Orchard, 2004)

W - *Wemberly Worried* by Kevin Henkes (Greenwillow, 2000)

Y - *Yoko* by Rosemary Wells (Hyperion, 1998)

Z - *Zathura* by Chris Van Allsburg (Houghton Mifflin, 2002)

Teaching Tip

When searching for book titles or characters from picture books to represent each letter of the alphabet, it is important to keep the letter sounds pure. For example, be aware that popular characters, such as Clifford, Franklin, and Froggy, are not good examples for the /k/ or /f/ sounds because they are blends, not single sounds.

Introducing bl- Blends

Explain that in some words two consonants appear beside each other at the beginning of the word. Start by teaching the bl- blend. Give hints to help students guess words that begin with the bl- blend, such as *black, blade, blank, blister,* and *blue.* For example, give the clue, "This word is a color, this word is part of a knife, etc." Title a piece of chart paper bl- Blends. As students guess the correct words, write them on chart paper under the title.

Extension - This guessing game is appropriate for introducing any set of blend or digraph words (see pages 135–136 for suggested words).

st- Blends

Copy the st- blends patterns, directions, and answer key (page 134). Glue the directions to the front of a file folder. Glue the answer key to the back. Cut out the patterns and glue them randomly to the inside of a file folder. Laminate the folder and place it at a center with a write-on/wipe-away marker. Ask students to write the letters *st* on the line in front of the picture if the word starts with that blend, or on the line behind the picture if the word ends with that blend. Picture names are *stinger, store, stage, stamp, stapler, star, toast, nest, vest, cast, list,* and *fist.*

Blends Name Game

After introducing several blends to students, including all of the blends used in students' first, middle, and last names, play the Blends Name Game. Write each student's first name on one index card, middle name on a second index card, and last name on a third card. Give the cards to the appropriate students. Consider making them into necklaces or taping them to students' shirts. Tell students to sort themselves into groups by finding other people in the class who have the same blends in their first names. Instruct students without first name blends to form a group, as well. For example, Stefan, Stella, and Austin should gather in a group; Brittany, Aubrey, and Brad should gather in a group; and La Shea, Yoshi, and Shane should gather in a group; while Tara, Juan, and Ali should be in a group of students with no blends in their names. Repeat with middle and last names.

Teaching Tip

The term *blend* means two adjacent consonant sounds. In a consonant blend, the sound of each letter is still heard, but they are blended together. *Digraph* is the linguistic term for two or more letters that are combined to represent one new sound, such as /sh/, /ch/, /th/, and /wh/. When most students have learned most of the single letter sounds, begin introducing letter blends and digraphs.

Directions: Look at each picture. Say its name. Write *st* on each line to make a word that begins or ends with that sound. Look at the back of the folder to check your work. When you are finished, use a damp tissue to erase what you wrote.

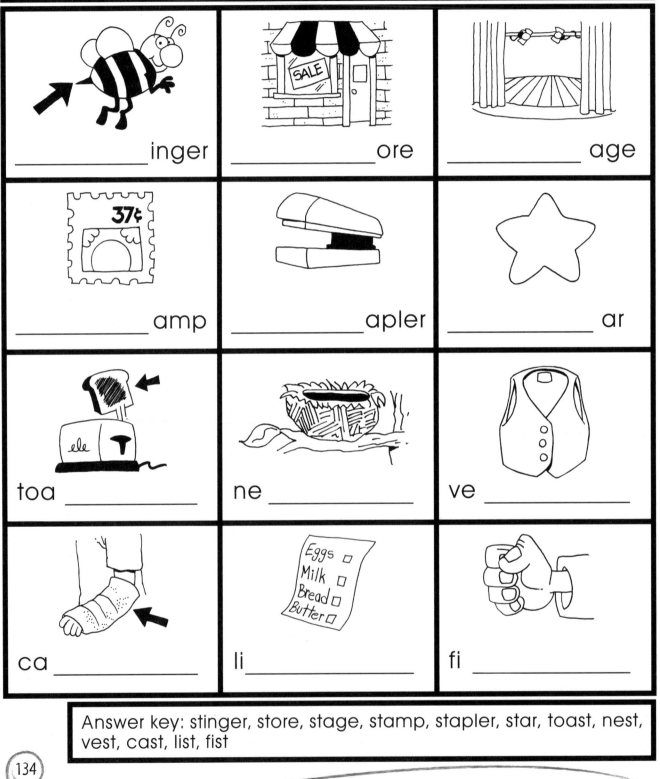

_____inger

_____ore

_____age

_____amp

_____apler

_____ar

toa _____

ne _____

ve _____

ca _____

li_____

fi _____

Answer key: stinger, store, stage, stamp, stapler, star, toast, nest, vest, cast, list, fist

Teacher's Helper: Two-Letter Initial Blend Words

bl– blade, black, blackbird, blank, blanket, blast, blaze, bleach, bleed, blend, blindfold, blister, blockbuster, blond, blink, bloom, blossom, blue

br– brace, brag, braid, brain, brake, branch, brand, brass, brat, brave, bread, breeze, bribe, brick, bride, bridge, bright, bring, broil, broom, brother, brow, brunch, brush

cl– clack, clam, clang, clarinet, class, claw, clay, clerk, click, clink, clip, clipboard, clock, clothes, cloud, clove, clown, clutch

cr– crab, crack, cracker, cradle, craft, cranberry, crank, crate, crayons, creak, creep, crib, cricket, crier, crisp, crocodile, crow, crowd, crown, crust, cry

dr– drab, drag, drain, dragon, draw, dream, dress, dried, drier, drift, drill, drink, drip, drive, drown, drum, dry, dryer

fl– flag, flame, flamingo, flap, flare, flashlight, flat, flea, flier, flight, flip, flirt, float, flock, Florida, floss, flower, flute, fly

fr– fraction, frail, frame, franc, freckles, freight train, freighter, free, fresh, freeze, fried, friend, fries, fright, fringe, Frisbee®, frog, frost, frosting, frown

gl– glad, glade, glance, glare, glass, glasses, glide, globe, gloss, glove, glow, glue

gr– grab, grade, grain, grapes, grasp, grass, grasshopper, gray, graze, green, greet, greeting, grill, grin, grind, grip, groom, ground, grow, growl, grump

pl– place, plain, plan, plane, plate, play, pledge, plow, plug, plum

pr– pretzel, price, pride, prize, prince, print, proud, prowl, prune

sc– scab, scale, scan, scarf, scold, score, scowl, scuff

sk– skate, skin, skirt, skunk, skip, sky, ski, skit

sl– slab, slacks, sled, sleep, sleeve, sleigh, slice, slick, slide, slim, sling, slingshot, Slinky®, slipper, sloppy, slouch, slow, slug, slum, slump, slush

sm– small, smell, smile, smock, smog, smooth, smudge, smug

sn–	snack, snag, snail, snake, snap, sneak, sneakers, sneeze, Snickers®, snob, snoop, snore, snow, snowball, snub, snug
sp–	space, spade, spare, spark, speak, spear, speech, speed, spell, spend, spike, spill, spin, spine, spoil, spool, spoon, sport, spot, spout, spur
st–	stack, staff, stage, stain, stair, stamp, stand, star, stare, start, state, stay, steer, stem, stick, sting, stomp, stone, stop, store, stork, storm, stove
sw–	swear, sweet, swim, swing, swipe, swoop, sworn
tr–	trace, track, trade, trail, train, trampoline, trap, trash, tray, treat, tree, tribe, trick, trim, troll, troops, trout, truck, true, trumpet, trust, try
wr–	wrapping paper, wring, wrist, write, writing, wrong

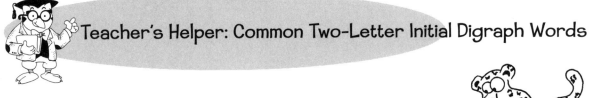

Teacher's Helper: Common Two-Letter Initial Digraph Words

ch–	chain, chair, chalk, chant, charge, charms, chart, chase, chat, cheap, checkbook, cheek, cheese, cheetah, cherry, chess, chest, chick, chicken, chill, chime, chimp, chin, chimpanzee, chip, chore
sh–	shack, shade, shake, shampoo, shape, share, shark, sharp, shave, shawl, shear, shed, sheep, sheet, shell, shield, shift, shin, shine, ship, shirt, shock, shoe, shop, shore
th–	thank, theft, thermometer, thigh, thin, thing, think, third, thorn, thumb
wh–	whale, wheat, while, whine, white, why

Teaching Tip

Different phonics programs treat the wh– digraph differently. Some programs do not consider it a digraph and treat the /wh/ sound as if it is pronounced like a /w/ sound.

Blend/Digraph Scavenger Hunt

Write common blends and digraphs on index cards. Post the cards in a pocket chart. Distribute blank index cards and markers to students, and instruct them to search signs, charts, and posters in the classroom for words that begin with those blends and digraphs. As they find these words, have students write them on the index cards and place them in the pocket chart to create a blend/digraph word wall. Periodically have a student select a word from the word wall, tell its meaning, say whether it contains a blend or a digraph, and explain her answer.

Sorting Pictures

Create a set of picture cards whose names represent two different beginning blends or digraphs. Either select several picture cards from this book, or create cards by cutting out small pictures from magazines and gluing them to index card. Put them in a resealable, plastic bag for easy access. Have pairs or small groups sort the pictures into two groups according to initial sounds of the names of the objects.

Extension – As students develop more advanced phonics and sorting skills, add more groups to the collection of picture cards.
Extension – Students can also sort pictures by ending sounds, medial sounds, number of syllables, and word families.

Same Sound – Different Sound

Explain that you will say two words. Then, call on a student. If the words begin with the same initial sound, the student should say, "Same sound." If the words begin with different sounds, the student should say, "Different sounds." Occasionally, ask a student to repeat the two initial sounds to justify his answer. Use this activity with blends and digraphs, with single consonant sounds, or with other sounds in words.

Extension – Play this game using same and different ending sounds.
Extension – Introduce two short vowel sounds and say pairs of three-letter words that do or do not have the same vowel sound. Students should respond with the above phrases and identify the vowel sound when the medial sounds are the same.

Teaching Tip

It is helpful to have a large collection of picture cards for sorting. Students can help create the cards. Stock a center with index cards, scissors, glue sticks, magazines, catalogs, and even phonics and spelling workbooks. Let students cut and paste pictures onto the index cards. Before assigning a sorting activity, let an adult volunteer sort the cards according to the criteria students will use to ensure that there are enough pictures that fit the designated criteria.

Mail Slot Phonics

Purchase a set of cardboard mailboxes with 8–10 slots from an office supply store. Or, create the structure by attaching open shoe boxes or other small boxes together. (Use only a few letters at a time, or create a full alphabet "mail" center.) Label each slot with a different letter by taping a small piece of paper with that letter written on it to the top of each slot. Provide a collection of picture cards with at least five cards per letter sound. Have students work together to sort the picture cards into the appropriate slots.

Extension – This picture card sorting activity relates to all sorts of language concepts. Consider playing this game with initial, medial, or ending sounds of words, or beginning blends or digraphs.

Teaching Tip

Letters and sounds for this activity can be chosen based on which letters students need more experiences with. See pages 31–32 for a form to help you document which students know which letters/sounds. To make "Mail Slot Phonics" sorting more realistic, place the picture cards in envelopes.

Assessment of Letter/Sound Recognition

Name _____ Date _____

Recorder _____

Use this form with the Assessment of Letter Recognition page (page 32). Ask the student to say the sound for each letter you point to. If you have taught alternative letter sounds (for a, c, e, g, i, o, q, u, and y), ask the student to name another sound that each of these letters makes sometimes. Circle the letter sounds correctly identified by the student. In the IR column, note any incorrect sounds the student says. After the assessment, make notes in the Comments and Reteaching Notes column.

Letters	Sound #1	Sound #2	Incorrect Response	Comments and Reteaching Notes
L	S1	S2	IR	CRN
A	short /a/	long /a/		
F	/f/			
K	/k/			
P	/p/			
U	short /u/	long /u/		
Z	/z/			
B	/b/			
G	/g/	/j/		
L	/l/			
Q	/kw/			
V	/v/			
C	/k/	/s/		
H	/h/			
M	/m/			
R	/r/			
W	/w/			
D	/d/			
I	short /i/	long /i/		
N	/n/			
S	/s/			
X	/ks/			
E	short /e/	long /e/		
J	/j/			
O	short /o/	long /o/		
T	/t/			
Y	long /i/	long /e/		

Teacher's Helper: Characters from Picture Books

Students often make connections between their lives and those of favorite characters in books they love. When you take time to establish a bond between students and a character, it creates one more opportunity to reinforce initial sounds by emphasizing the character's name.

A - Alexander from *Alexander and the Terrible, Horrible, No Good, Very Bad Day* by Judith Viorst (Atheneum, 1972)
Adelita from *Adelita: A Mexican Cinderella Story* by Tomie dePaola (Puffin, 2004)
Abiyoyo from *Abiyoyo* by Pete Seeger (Aladdin, 1994)
Amelia Bedelia from *Amelia Bedelia* by Peggy Parish (HarperTrophy, 1992)

B - Boris Beaver from *Boris Beaver* by Marcus Pfister (North-South Books, 1989)
Bobby from *Now One Foot, Now the Other* by Tomie dePaola (Putnam, 1981)
Little Bear from *Little Bear* by Else Holmelund Minarik (HarperTrophy, 1957)
Ben from *Ben's Trumpet* by Rachel Isadora (HarperTrophy, 1991)

C - Corduroy from *Corduroy* by Don Freeman (Viking Juvenile, 1968)
Cecilia from *A Birthday Basket for Tía* by Pat Mora (Aladdin, 1997)

D - Desta from *Faraway Home* by Jane Kurtz (Gulliver, 2000)
Daisy from *Daisy Comes Home* by Jan Brett (Putnam, 2002)
Daniel from *Daniel's Dinosaurs* by Mary Carmine (Scholastic, 1993)

E - Elvirey from *The Log Cabin Quilt* by Ellen Howard (Holiday House, 1996)
The Little Engine from *The Little Engine That Could* by Watty Piper (Grosset & Dunlap, 1978)

F - Fernando from *Fernando's Gift* by Douglas Keister (Sierra Club Books for Children, 1998)
Farfallina from *Farfallina & Marcel* by Holly Keller (Greenwillow, 2002)

G - George from *George and Martha* by James Marshall (Houghton Mifflin, 1997)
Gertrude from *Bonjour, Mr. Satie* by Tomie dePaola (Putnam, 1991)

H - Horton from *Horton Hatches the Egg* and *Horton Hears a Who!* by Dr. Seuss (Random House, 1940, 1954)
Harold from *Harold and the Purple Crayon* by Crockett Johnson (HarperCollins, 1955)
Heckedy Peg from *Heckedy Peg* by Audrey Wood (Harcourt Children's Books, 1987)
Harry from *Harry the Dirty Dog* by Gene Zion HarperCollins, 1956)

I – Imogene from *Imogene's Antlers* by David Small (Dragonfly Books, 1988)

Ira from *Ira Says Goodbye* by Bernard Waber (Houghton Mifflin, 1988)

J – Jimmy from *The Day Jimmy's Boa Ate the Wash* by Trinka Hakes Noble (Dial, 1980)

Jenna from *Jingle Dancer* by Cynthia Leitich Smith (HarperCollins, 2000)

Jesse Bear from *Jesse Bear, What Will You Wear?* by Nancy White Carlstrom (Simon & Schuster, 1986)

K – Kyla from *Do Like Kyla* by Angela Johnson (Scholastic, 1993)

Kenyon from *Keepers* by Jeri Hanel Watts (Lee & Low Books, 1987)

Koko from *Koko's Kitten* by Dr. Francine Patterson (Scholastic, 1987)

L – Leo from *Leo the Late Bloomer* by Robert Kraus (HarperCollins, 1971)

Lilly from *Lilly's Purple Plastic Purse* by Kevin Henkes (Greenwillow, 1996)

M – Mike Mulligan from *Mike Mulligan and His Steam Shovel* by Virginia Lee Burton (Houghton Mifflin, 1939)

Minty from *Minty: A Story of Young Harriet Tubman* by Alan Schroeder (Puffin, 2000)

N – Nora from *Noisy Nora* by Rosemary Wells (Viking Books, 1999)

Nate from *Nate the Great* by Marjorie Weinman Sharmat (Yearling, 1977)

Miss Nelson from *Miss Nelson is Missing* by Harry Allard and James Marshall (Houghton Mifflin, 1985)

O – Opus from *Goodnight Opus* by Berkeley Breathed (Little, Brown, 1996)

Olivia from *Olivia* by Ian Falconer (Atheneum, 2000)

Omar from *Save My Rainforest* by Monica Zak (Volcano Press, 1992)

R – Rosie from *Rosie's Walk* by Pat Hutchins (Aladdin, 1971)

Richard from *My Rotten Redheaded Older Brother* by Patricia Polacco (Aladdin, 1998)

S – Sal from *Blueberries for Sal* by Robert McCloskey (Viking Juvenile, 1948)

Sam from *Sam, Bangs and Moonshine* by Evaline Ness (Henry Holt and Co., 1971)

T – Taro from *The Boy of the Three-Year Nap* by Dianne Snyder (Houghton Mifflin, 1993)

Tony from *Tony's Bread* by Tomie dePaola (Putnam, 1996)

Tikki Tikki Tembo from *Tikki Tikki Tembo* by Arlene Mosel (Henry Holt and Co., 1968)

V – Victor from *Babushka Baba Yaga* by Patricia Polacco (Putnam, 1999)

Vladimir from *Wake Up, Vladimir!* by Felicia Bond (Ty Crowell Co., 1987)

W – Wodney Wat from *Hooway for Wodney Wat* by Helen Lester (Houghton Mifflin, 2002)

Winston from *Chicken Sunday* by Patricia Polacco (Putnam, 1998)

Y – Yunmi from *Yunmi and Halmoni's Trip* by Sook Nyul Choi (Houghton Mifflin, 1997)

Yoko from *Yoko* by Rosemary Wells (Hyperion, 1998)

Yertle from *Yertle the Turtle* by Dr. Seuss (Random House, 1958)

Z – Zomo from *Zomo the Rabbit: A Trickster Tale from West Africa* retold by Gerald McDermott (Voyager, 1996)

Zack from *Zack's Alligator* by Shirley Mozelle (HarperTrophy, 1995)

Teacher's Helper: Anchor Experiences for Remembering Letter Sounds

Kinesthetic learners tend to associate letter sounds with activities they have helped to create. For example, kinesthetic learners will better remember the /h/ sound after making handprints on hats. Below are several suggestions for building, making, or creating experiences related to each letter of the alphabet. (Before completing any food activity, be sure to get families' permission and check for allergies and religious or other preferences.) Depending on students' needs, you may choose to leave out activities starting with blends, digraphs, or r-controlled vowels.

A Make aluminum foil sculptures. Suggest that students think of and sculpt objects that start with short or long /a/, such as alligators, ants, apes, etc. ● Make apple prints by cutting apples in half and letting students dip them in green, red, or yellow paint and then stamp them on paper. ● Have an art show. Let students choose their best pieces of art to post around the classroom. Invite families or other classes to view the art show.

B Have a book share. Let each student bring in a favorite book to share. ● Make bracelets using beads. ● Create a make-believe center with beanbag babies (stuffed-animal beanbags). ● Make bubble solution and bubble wands. To make bubble solution, combine 1 part dish detergent, 15 parts water, and .25 parts glycerine. To make wands, bend wire coat hangers into rounded shapes. Cover the sharp ends of the hangers with heavy plastic bags and tape to make handles. Pour the solution into large, shallow containers and let students make bubbles.

C Create colorful collages from construction paper. ● Study castles and build one from large cardboard containers, such as boxes that held furniture, appliances, or electronics. ● Make colorful coasters by tracing and cutting out circles from construction paper. Let students decorate the circles, then laminate them.

D Design drums from coffee cans or oatmeal boxes, let students decorate them, then play music with a strong beat so that students can play along with their drums. ● Teach students about the didgeridoo, a native Australian instrument with an interesting construction and unusual sound. ● Have a classroom dance party. Put on child-appropriate music and teach students your favorite dance steps.

E   Boil and dye eggs, then have hard–boiled egg races by letting students carry the eggs in spoons from a starting point to a finish line.

F   Let students finger paint. ● Plant flowers in pots or on the playground. ● Let students make fans by coloring pictures on white paper and then accordion-folding the paper and stapling it at the bottom. ● Create fingertip puppets by cutting apart cardboard egg carton cups and letting students add facial features with markers. ● Help students make their own fingerprints using ink pads and white paper.

G   Create a mysterious "gloop" using cornstarch and water. Mix the two together until they form a paste that is solid when pressure is applied, but is otherwise runny.
    ● Check out and share books about gargoyles, the mysterious, carved creatures that act as building drainpipes. (Note that similar figures not used as drainpipes are often called gargoyles, but are more properly called *grotesques*.) ● Have a glove day on which students wear gloves as they try to do their daily tasks in the classroom. Discuss which tasks are easier and which are more difficult with gloves.

H   Create hats from sentence strips and let students decorate them.
    ● Create handprint art by letting each student press her hands in paint and then on a paper-covered bulletin board. Label and date each student's handprints.

I   Build igloos from gallon milk jugs, sugar cubes, papier-mâché, etc. ● Have an ice cream party. Provide ice cream, syrup, whipped topping, banana slices, nuts, etc., and let students build their own ice cream sundaes. (Before completing any food activity, be sure to get families' permission and check for food allergies and religious or other preferences.)

J   Make jewelry or junk sculptures from found objects. ● Have a jumping rope or jumping jacks contest.
    ● Have a joke day. Teach students about different types of jokes and let students tell jokes to the class.

K   Go fly kites! On a windy day, take students to an open area and fly kites. ● Make key chains from metal rings. Let each student attach a few objects to her key chain, such as ribbons or string, paper clips, etc., to personalize it. Send home the key chains for families to use to hold extra keys.

L   Make leaf prints by pressing leaves into paint and then onto paper. ● Have a limbo contest. Bring a broom to class and play party music. Let students form a line and take turns bending backwards under the broom handle as they walk under it. Lower the broom a little each time. ● Students often like to make lists. Have them help you brainstorm lists for several different topics, such as what games they would like to play at recess, what gifts they would like for their birthdays, etc.

143

M Let students make masks from paper plates and art supplies. ● Make *maracas* using plastic containers with lids and dried beans. Let students decorate their maracas and then play mariachi music. Encourage students to play along.

N Make N necklaces. On construction paper, have each student trace and cut out a letter *N* and then tape it to a yarn necklace. Tie the string and let students wear their necklaces for the rest of the school day. ● Make number art. Provide a large sheet of paper and art supplies for each student. Let her write numbers from 0-10 on the paper using markers, crayons, glitter glue, paint, etc. ● Ask students to bring in newspapers. Demonstrate how to fold newspaper hats.

O Play opera music for the class and ask students to describe what they think is happening during different songs. ● Let students make collages with ovals and octagons. ● Create an obstacle course and use position words that begin with the letter *o* (*on, over, out, outside*, etc.) to direct students as they go through the course. ● Choose a day for students to wear orange clothing, drink orange juice, and eat orange foods (cheese, cantaloupe, etc.). (When planning a food activity, be sure to get families' permission and check for food allergies and religious or other preferences.)

P Make play dough by mixing four cups of flour, one cup of salt, four cups of water, four tablespoons of vegetable oil, and one-half cup of cream of tartar in a saucepan. Cook over low heat until the dough comes together and is not sticky. Allow it to cool and store it in an airtight container when not in use. ● Let students make paper bag puppets from lunch bags and markers. Let them glue on yarn hair. ● Enjoy a puzzle week. Set up card tables with simple jigsaw puzzles. Let a few students at a time rotate to the tables to work on the puzzles. ● Provide a *piñata* that has streamers to pull to empty the contents. Fill it with appropriate food and small toys. (Before completing any food activity, be sure to get families' permission and check for food allergies and religious or other preferences.)

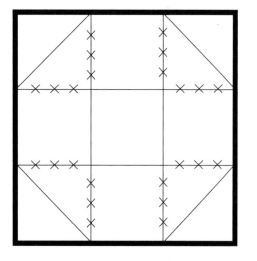

Q Have students make quilt squares. Enlarge the quilt square pattern (right) for each student. Allow each student to decorate his square with a self-portrait, then connect all of the squares with yarn on a bulletin board to make a class quilt. ● Let students paint pictures using Q-tips® and tempera paint.

R   Collect rocks on the playground or have students bring them from home to start a class rock collection.
● Provide dark crayons and paper and have students go outside to make rubbings of different surfaces, such as tree bark, brick or stone walls, etc., with the sides of the crayons. (Make sure students know not to color the surfaces, but to rub only the paper with the sides of the crayons.)

S   Encourage students to create snakes from clay or play dough. ● Plan activities with sand. Fill shoe box lids with sand and have students trace words that begin with the letter *s*. Provide small, clear, plastic soda bottles and small packages of colorful sand for students to layer in the bottles. Let students use colorful sand, paper, and glue to make sand paintings.

T   Talk about turtles. Let students cut out legs, heads, and tails from green construction paper, then have them add features with markers. Let each student paint the bottom of a small paper plate to look like a turtle shell, then glue her turtle parts to the underside of the plate. ● Provide old mobile phones, regular phones, and toy telephones and let students pretend to talk on the telephones.

U   Ask students to bring in umbrellas. Go outside and dance with them on a rainy (but not stormy) day.

V   Create vests. Provide a paper grocery bag for each student. Cut each bag up the center on one side and then cut holes for arms. Let students decorate their vests, then wear them as they learn the /v/ sound.

W   Ask students to bring in cereal boxes, then attach them with glue or tape to build a giant wall in the classroom. Leave gaps in the wall for windows.
● Make place mats from waxed paper. Let students place crayon shavings between two sheets of the paper. Paperclip the edges together and write students' names in the corners. Have an adult take home the place mats, place each student's place mat on an ironing board, cover it with a towel, and iron over the towel on the lowest setting.
● Let students make wind chimes from donated bent forks and spoons, shells, jingle bells, etc. Go outside on a windy day to test out the chimes.

X   Teach students how to play tic-tac-toe, making sure they can draw the letter X and say its sound.
   ● Hide small toys or other surprises around the classroom. Create a rough map of the classroom, copy it a few times, and draw an X in a different spot on each map. Assign students to small groups and let each group find a hidden surprise. Explain that X marks the spot where each group will find a treasure.

Y   Let students make yarn paintings by dipping strands of yarn into paint and then dragging the yarn across pieces of paper.

Z   Create a classroom zoo mural. ● Show students how to draw a zigzag line. Let students make collages of zigzag lines using markers, paint, crayons, rickrack, etc.

● ● Where Does the Sound Go?

Give each student two blank letter tiles and one letter tile with a consonant written on it. Say a series of words with no more than three phonemes that contain that consonant. Have students push tiles up on the table so that one represents each phoneme (not letter) in the word. See possible examples below. As students master three-phoneme words, add another blank letter tile, then another as students are ready.

it – blank, t	be – b, blank
tie – t, blank	by – b, blank
tame – t, blank, blank	bed – b, blank, blank
bat – blank, blank, t	bat – b, blank, blank
kite – blank, blank, t	crab – blank, blank, blank, b
tapes – t, blank, blank, blank	grabs – blank, blank, blank, b, blank
locket – blank, blank, blank, blank, t	basket – b, blank, blank, blank, blank, blank

Extension – After students master words with five phonemes, add an additional consonant tile so that students are using multiple consonants and multiple unknown phonemes.

Guess My Rule

Write 15-20 short words on large index cards and place them in a pocket chart. Select two or three words with a common characteristic, such as same initial letter or final letter. As you move these cards to an empty area of the pocket chart, challenge students by saying, "Guess my rule." Ask them to identify the common characteristic and add words to the group that follow that "rule." As students guess the rule, they should say, "Is the rule _____?" Answer, "That's not my rule," or "That is my rule." If students are stuck, give clues to help them along.

Extension – Sort cards into two categories and have students guess the two categories. Possible clues for "rules" categories could include words with the short /e/ sound versus short /a/ sound, words with bl– blend versus words without the bl– blend, rhyming words versus words that do not rhyme, same rime versus different rimes, and so on.

Teacher's Helper: More about Informal Assessment

Sometimes assessment forms help focus our attention on the specific skills we want to observe in our students. As stated on page 8, instead of using a formal assessment, sometimes it is necessary to evaluate students on an individual basis. For example, if you need to document which letters a child can name, it is most time efficient to go through all 52 letters with each student and complete a checklist as the child responds to prompts. At these times, you need to set up engaging activities for the rest of the class so that you are free to talk with one child at a time. However, it is not always necessary to meet with each child individually. Some literacy-related skills do not require this type of formal assessment. Certain skills such as phonological awareness can be documented in a more informal way. As you watch children interact with each other during an activity or as they play games, you can make notes about the rhyming words they mention or the words they mention that begin with the same initial consonant sound. Both carefully structured and informal assessment methods can be effective. Just decide which way works best for the skills you need to assess.

Assessment for Initial and Final Sounds of Words

Use the forms on pages 148-149 to assess whether students have mastered these skills. Fill out a form with name, date, and name of recorder for each student. Consider using an adult volunteer to help you assess all students' progress. Use the results on the forms to plan reteaching of these skills.

147

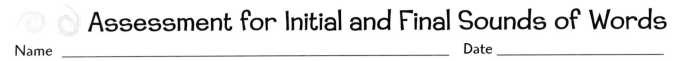

Assessment for Initial and Final Sounds of Words

Name _____ Date _____

Recorder _____

Use this assessment with a copy of the Word List: Assessment for Initial and Final Sounds of Words (page 149). Show the student one word at a time. If the student can name the initial sound, put a check mark in the IS column next to the word. Next, have the student identify the final sound and put a check under the FS column if the student is able to do so. If the student gives an incorrect response, put a check under the IR column, and then record what that response was in the SR column.

WL (Word List, see page 149)	IS (Identifies Initial Sound)	FS (Identifies Final Sound)	IR (Gives Incorrect Response)	SR (Student Response)
cat				
fan				
dog				
fox				
ball				
cloud				
dragon				
stop				
bath				
song				

cat

fan

dog

fox

ball

cloud

dragon

stop

bath

song

Onset and Rime

Onset and rime are terms used to describe phonological units of a spoken syllable. A syllable can normally be divided into two parts: the onset, which consists of the initial consonant or consonant blend, and the rime, which consists of the vowel and any final consonants. For example, in the word *cat*, c is the onset and –at is the rime. In the word *slight*, sl is the onset and –ight is the rime. Words which do not share the same rime can also rhyme, but in a rime the spelling is constant and does not vary (as in *big* and *dig*) like it does with other words that simply rhyme (as in *hare* and *pair*).

The importance of understanding onset and rime in the process of learning to read and later in learning to spell was well-documented by multiple studies in the 1980s. These studies support the idea that teaching students to pay attention to onset and rime in unknown words has a positive affect on their literacy skills. Generally, students quickly pick up the understanding that if they know how to pronounce and spell one word with a rime, they can pronounce and spell other words with that same rime. If a student reads the word *cat*, she then uses that knowledge to decode and read the words *bat* and *hat* because they use the same rime. This is considered the strategy of analogy. Students who have difficulty learning to read and spell often have poor phonological awareness; they do not naturally use analogy and must be taught this skill. Teaching students the concept that words which share common sounds often share spellings is a powerful tool to help them on their way to literacy.

Multisensory methods should be used to teach onset and rime, including significant time spent in kinesthetic activities. Teaching short lessons every day is more beneficial than teaching one long lesson once a week. The same target rimes normally must be taught and reviewed several times, so this section includes multiple ways to teach specific onsets and rimes. Most activities can easily be modified to teach a variety of onsets and rimes.

The Truck Is Loaded With . . .

Ask a small group of students to sit in a circle. Begin the game by saying, "The truck is loaded with frogs." Toss a beanbag to a student and ask him to make a rhyme with the beginning sentence, such as "The truck is loaded with logs (dogs, hogs, jogs, pogs, etc.)." (Accept nonsense words as long as they rhyme.) Continue until the group cannot think of any more rhymes.

Hop on Pop

Read Dr. Seuss's book *Hop on Pop* (Random House, 1963). Write the following sentences on sentence strips and display them.

- We like to h--.
- We like to h-- on t-- of P--.
- St--, you must not h-- on P--.

Have students practice blending the phonemes together before reading the sentences. Have the class read the sentences and say /op/ wherever they see the blanks. After students are proficient in reading the sentences, give student volunteers a pointer and ask them to use it to guide each other as they practice reading the sentences aloud.

Extension – Almost any book that features rhythm and rhyme can be used to focus on one rime. Choose one rime from the book. Create two or three sentences that use the rime and three or four different onsets. Then, go through the same procedure shown in this activity.

 Taking a Trip

On poster board, create a game board by drawing square spaces in the shape of a winding trail, or enlarge one of the generic game boards from this book (pages 96-97). Copy the sign patterns (page 152) and glue them at different points along the trail. On each sign, write a rime of common word families, such as -ap, -at, -ed, -en, -ig, -op, and -ot. Have two students take turns rolling a die and moving a game piece that many spaces. When a game piece lands on a square that has a sign beside it, the player must stop and say (or write) a rhyming word for that rime. Be sure to put a sign at the end so that students must make a final rhyme to win the game.

> ## Teaching Tip
>
> Laminate the game poster board, then let students use write-on/wipe-away pens to write the rhyming words on the game board. After students have finished playing, have them use a damp tissue to erase the words.

151

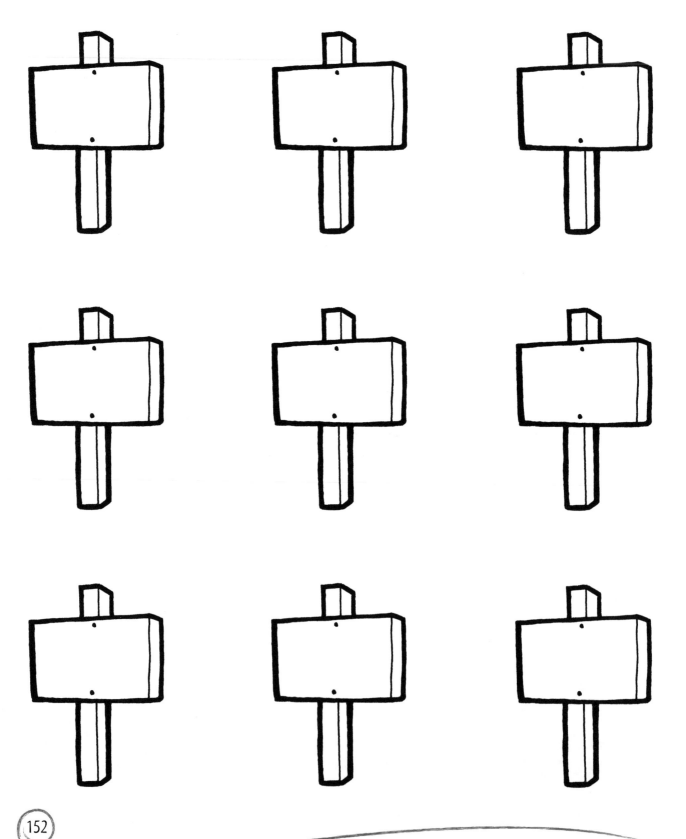

Rhyming Lunches

Copy the place settings (page 155), then color them, cut them out, and glue them to the inside of a file folder. Copy, color, and cut out the bread, tomato, and cheese patterns, along with the directions and answer key (pages 154–155). Glue the directions to the front of the folder. Store the answer key with the remaining patterns. Have students use the matching pictures to build four different rhyme sandwiches and put them on plates. To make additional games, cover the word families and words on the pattern pieces before copying them, then copy and use the blank patterns. Write different word endings on the plates, then glue pictures or write word family words on the bread, tomato, and cheese patterns.

The Flower Garden

This game will help students' word family knowledge grow. Copy, color, and cut out the flower and stem patterns (page 156). Write an onset on each flower. On each stem, write a rime that creates a word when matched to an onset on a flower. Glue the stems to the inside of a file folder. Store the flowers in a resealable, plastic bag. Copy and glue the directions to the front of the folder. Create an answer key to make the activity self-checking and store it with the flowers. Ask students to "grow" flowers by matching each onset and rime.

Rodeo Time

Copy and color the cowboy and cowgirl patterns (pages 157–158). Copy and cut out the boot patterns, directions, and answer key. Glue the directions to the front of the folder. Store the boot patterns and answer key together. Have students play the game by letting Tex and Dot "try on" boots to see if they make words that begin with the letters *t* and *d*, respectively. Use the blank boots to add any words you wish for students to learn. Note that *din* and *tin* are both words, although students may not recognize them.

Humpty Dumpty Take-Off

Repeat a familiar nursery rhyme. Ask students to "take off" the onset of a word and pronounce the remaining rime. For example, after reciting "Humpty Dumpty," say, "Take off the /w/ sound in *wall* and you have *all*. Take off the /h/ sound in *horses* and you have *orses*. Take off the /k/ sound in *king's* and you have *ings*. Take off the /m/ sound in *men* and you have *en*." Let students select other words from the rhyme and remove their onsets.

Extension – Play this game after a read-aloud. Use story words for the onset and rime segmenting.

153

Rhyming Lunches

Directions: Help make sandwiches for lunch. Each sandwich must have two slices of bread, a slice of tomato, and a slice of cheese. Make sure that the pictures on each sandwich rhyme. Place the finished sandwiches on their matching plates.

Answer Key

On -at plate: bat, cat, mat, hat
On -eel plate: eel, heel, seal, wheel
On -ock plate: rock, clock, sock, lock
On -ug plate: bug, mug, rug, slug

© Carson-Dellosa • CD-104165

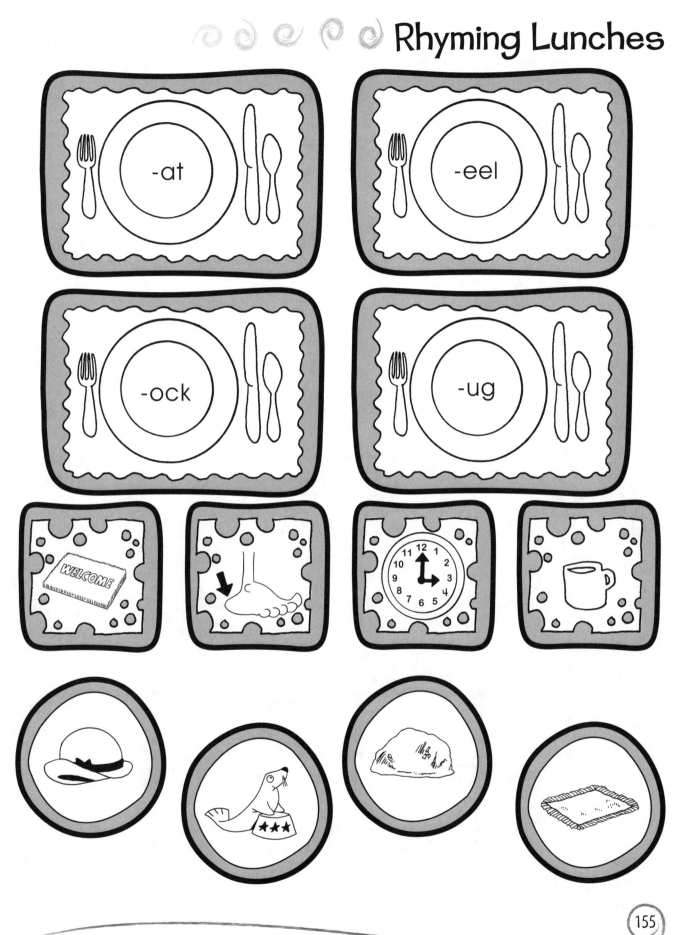

The Flower Garden

Directions: Grow some flowers in your garden. Match each flower to a stem to make a word.

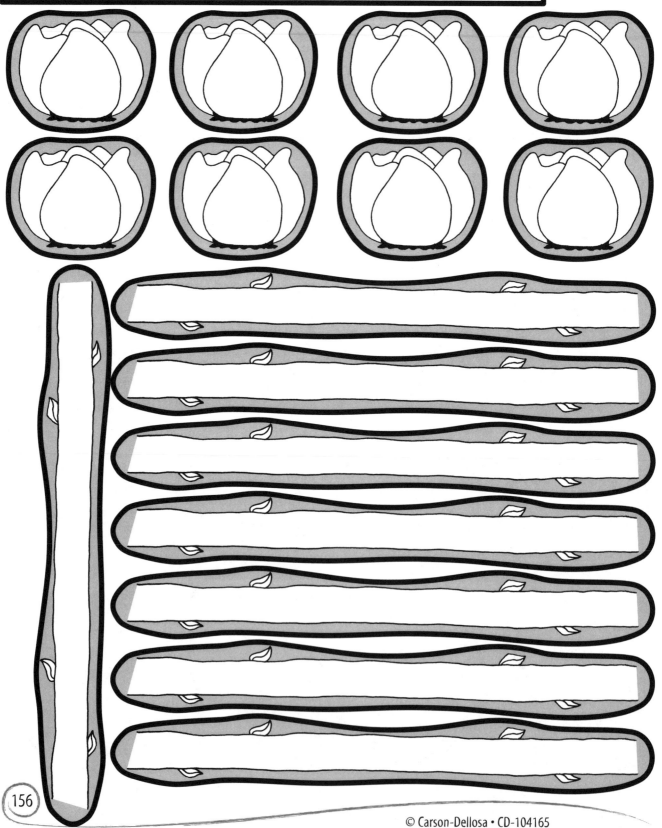

Directions: Tex and Dot are getting ready for the rodeo. Tex only wears boots that have letters on them that can make words that begin with the /t/ sound. Dot only wears boots that have letters on them that can make words that begin with the /d/ sound. Take turns choosing boots for them to wear. If a word could start with /t/, place the boot next to Tex. If a word could start with /d/, place the boot next to Dot.

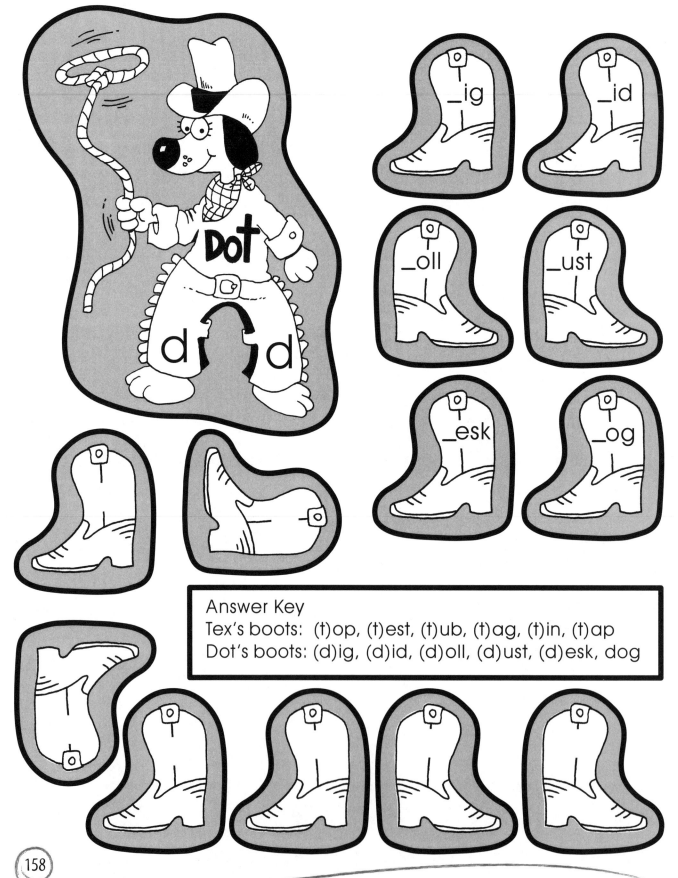

Answer Key
Tex's boots: (t)op, (t)est, (t)ub, (t)ag, (t)in, (t)ap
Dot's boots: (d)ig, (d)id, (d)oll, (d)ust, (d)esk, dog

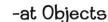

Word Parts Puzzles

Write parts of words such as *b-at, c-at, p-ig, b-ig, f-an, b-all, d-og, f-ish, b-ook,* and *c-ook* on different-colored index cards. Put the onsets on one color of card, and the rimes on a different color. Mix up the cards and put them in a shallow box or large, resealable plastic bag. Have students work in pairs or groups of three. Let them take turns choosing one card of each color at random. During his turn, the student should put the word parts together and blend them to determine whether the word is a real word or not. If the two parts make a real word, the student should keep those cards. If the two parts do not make a real word, he should return the cards to the box. The student with the most real words is the winner. (Other possible words from the combinations listed include *bog, call, can, Dan, dig, dish, fall, fat, fig, fog, pan,* and *pat.*)

-at Objects

Copy and cut out the bat, cat, hat, and mat patterns, along with the directions and answer key (page 160). Write *–at* on the blank in the directions. Glue the -at patterns to the inside of a file folder. Write ___at under each card. Color the directions and glue them to the front of a file folder. Laminate the folder. Let students take turns using a write-on/wipe-away pen to write each correct onset in front of the rimes.

Extension – Use the additional patterns (pages 160-161) to create many versions of this file folder activity. Modify the directions (page 160) by writing different rimes (word families) in the blanks and under the cards. Let students write in the correct onsets. Store each answer key with its corresponding words.

Page	Rimes	Object names
160-161	-ail	mail, nail, sail, snail, tail
161	-an	can, fan, man, pan, van
161	-ing	king, ring, sling, swing, wing
161	-og	dog, frog, hog, log
161	-ot	cot, dot, knot, spot

Onset/Rime Sorting

Give students additional word family practice. Make an additional set of the onset/rime patterns (pages 160-161), and copy the Onset/Rime Sorting directions and answer key (page 160). Let students color the pictures. (Do not write the onsets or rimes on the cards.) Write each of the word families listed above on an index card to create a set of six cards. Laminate the index cards, patterns, and answer keys, and store them in an envelope. Let pairs or small groups of students take turns placing the index cards in a row and sorting the pictures under their correct word families. Be sure to check students' work when they are finished sorting.

159

_____ Objects Directions: Write the first letter to make a word from the word family. Look at each picture to help you decide which letter to write.

Onset/Rime Sorting Directions: Place the index cards in a line. Sort the pictures under the index cards into the correct word families.

Answer key for _ at: bat, cat, hat, mat

Answer key for _ ail: mail, nail, sail, snail, tail

Answer key for _ an: can, fan, man, pan, van

Answer key for _ ing: king, ring, sling, swing, wing

Answer key for _ og: dog, frog, hog, log

Answer key for _ ot: cot, dot, knot, spot

Word Webs

Write one rime in the center of a large piece of paper and underline it in one color. Ask students to brainstorm words that end with that rime. Write their words around the rime. Use the same color to underline the rime in each new word written on the poster. Ask students to volunteer to sketch a simple drawing for each word on the word web.

Extension – Word webs can also be created using an onset at the center of the poster, with brainstormed words written and illustrated around the onset.

Word Wheels

Enlarge the Word Wheel patterns (pages 163–165) onto card stock. Cut out the patterns, including the wedge shape in each onset wheel. Attach the two patterns by lining up the centers and joining them with a paper fastener. Demonstrate how to spin the wheels to make new words using the same onset.

Extension – After students have had multiple opportunities to work with the word wheels, provide copies of the blank wheel templates (page 164) on card stock for students to design their own word wheels.

Explain-the-Word Cards

To make this card set, acquire two sets of index cards, each a different color. For example, use a blue set and a pink set. On the blue set, use blue ink to write word families that students are studying. In front of each ending, draw an underline in red to indicate that other letters should go there. Cut one-third off of each card in the pink set. In red, on the one-third portion of each card, write all of the consonants, blends, and digraphs. Work in a center with one to three students. Let each student take a turn matching a pink beginning card with a blue ending card. Help her explain the subsequent word she makes. Record all of the words and a brief definition (supplied by the student) on chart paper. If the student makes a nonsense word, work with the student to say the word and then help her choose an alternative. As students learn more word families, add more blue ending cards to the set.

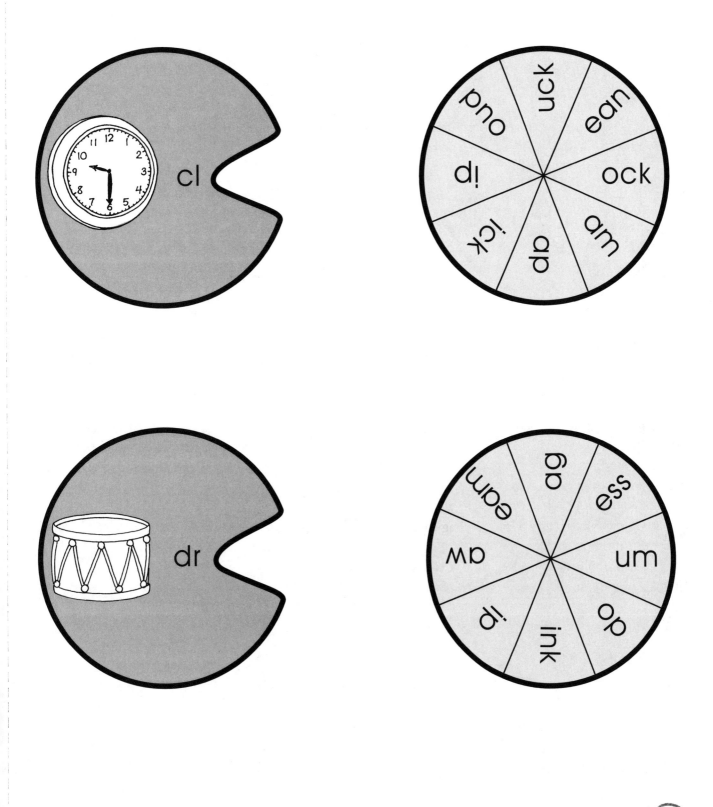

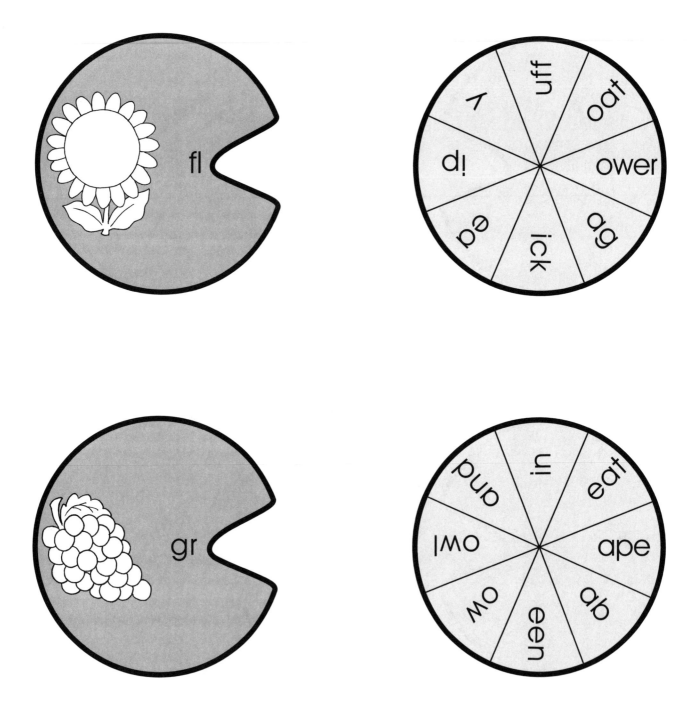

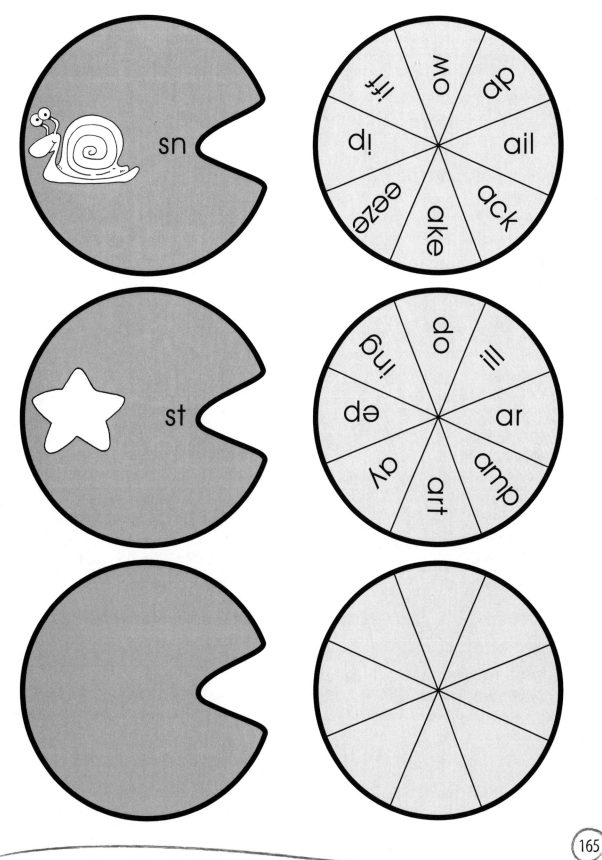

sn

st

mo

ap

iff

ail

di

ack

eeze

ake

do

ill

ing

ar

de

amp

by

art

Odd Man Out

Recite a list of words that end with the same rime. Insert one word with a different rime. For example, say, "Jump, pump, dump, gum, lump, stump." (Make the stand-out word more obvious if students need an easier challenge.) When you have completed the list, raise your hand and have students respond in unison by calling out the word with the different rime.

Jack and Jill and the Hill

Chant the traditional rhyme, then say it again with emphasis on the -ill rime. Challenge students to call out more words with -ill rimes, such as *bill, chill, drill, fill*, etc. Repeat the nursery rhyme, but focus on different words to emphasize the rimes -ack, -ail, -ell, and –oke. Brainstorm more rimes for those as well.

Jack and Jill
Went up the hill,
To fetch a pail of water.
Jack fell down,
And broke his crown,
And Jill came tumbling after.

Extension – Change some of the lines to emphasize other rimes. For example:

Jon and Pat
Got a pet cat,
And took him to their home.
They bathed him well,
To get rid of the smell,
Then groomed him with a comb.

Assessment for Onsets and Rimes

Make a copy of the Assessment for Onsets and Rimes (page 167) for each student. To assess onsets, say the first five groups of words and fill in the sheet according to students' answers. Repeat for rimes using the next five sets.

Assessment for Onsets and Rimes

Name _____

Recorder _____

Use this form to document students' abilities to hear onsets and rimes. When you observe children accomplishing the following skills, make a note in that column of the day's date and document what the child said or did to prove competence in these skills.

Date	Identifies Common Onset	Identifies Word with Different Onset	Incorrect Response	Notes for Reteaching
D	CO	DO	IR	R

- -

Date	Identifies Common Rime	Identifies Word with Different Rime	Incorrect Response	Notes for Reteaching
D	CR	DR	IR	R

Blending

Blending sounds is another form of phonemic awareness. It is the ability to recognize and manipulate individual sounds in words; that is, to smoothly join phonemes to come up with a pronunciation close enough to a word to access the word. To blend phonemes, students must "combine individual phonemes to form words," or "combine onsets and rimes to make syllables or combine syllables to make words" (CIERA, 2001). Note that blending phonemes also can mean being able to add new phonemes to words or substitute one or more phonemes for another, and then blend them with existing phonemes in that word. Learning to blend phonemes is the basic skill underlying the encouraging statement, "Sound it out," that many young students hear as they are learning to read. Obviously, to blend sounds, students must know the sounds associated with each letter of the alphabet as well as blends and digraphs.

Young students are usually introduced to blending through rhyming. Rhyming is essentially blending a new onset to an old rime. Students should not be expected to produce rhymes until they have much experience recognizing rimes. Listening to rhyming stories, reciting rhyming poetry, and singing rhyming songs should be daily activities in the early childhood classroom. Students can first try making rhymes by blending a single onset to a variety of words.

Instruction in decoding begins as soon as students know enough sounds to make words. For example, if students know the sounds /k/, /a/, and /t/, they can be taught to blend those sounds and read the words *at* and *cat*.

Perhaps one of the easiest ways to introduce blending to young students is to start with familiar word families like –at. From –at, students can be led through blending the onsets of b-, c-, f-, h-, m-, p-, and s- to the rime –at.

Onset/Rime Puzzles

Copy the Puzzle patterns (page 169-171) onto colorful card stock. Cut out the individual cards and cut each one apart on the dotted lines. Laminate the pieces. Put the puzzle pieces on the floor. Model for a small group how to search for matching pieces. When a student finds a match, he should announce the onset letter sound, then the rime, and then put the two pieces together to say the entire word.

Extension – Select a few words for the Onset/Rime puzzles. Enlarge the sketches onto large pieces of poster board. Distribute half of a puzzle to each student, ask him to find the student with other half of his puzzle, and then stand side-by-side with his classmate to make a word.

c|at

d|og

f|ish

p|ig

d|uck

h|at

b|at

b|all

n et

sh oe

s ock

c ake

r ake

b ell

w ing

r ing

n|ail

s|ail

b|us

n|est

fr|og

p|an

f|eet

b|ed

m|oon

sp|oon

cl|ock

l|ock

ga|te

s|un

st|ar

c|ar

● ● Putting the Sounds Together

Within a small group, choose one student and say each of the phonemes in his name very slowly. Pause briefly between each phoneme so that the sounds are isolated. Challenge group members to identify whose name you are saying. If more than one student's name begins with the same sound, it is okay for students to begin guessing the name with the first sound, but encourage them to wait until they hear all of the sounds.

> **Teaching Tip**
>
> Blending isolated sounds together to make a word is not an easy skill to learn. The task is easier when students are particularly interested in the words that are being created.

● ● Say it Faster, Move it Closer

Choose a three-letter word with three phonemes. Place two letter manipulatives to represent the first two letters (a consonant and a vowel), far apart on a table. Point to the consonant and have students say the sound of that letter. Have them continue making the sound until you move your finger to the vowel. Then, have students pronounce the sound of that letter as well. Move the letters closer together and repeat the procedure so that students pronounce the sounds a little faster. Move the letters together until they are touching as you and students say the two sounds as one unit. Add a final consonant and repeat the activity with the first two sounds still together as you and students blend the three sounds to form a word.

● ● Bookmarking Words

Create a list of 10-12 three-letter words. On lined handwriting paper, write the words so that there is about half an inch of space between each letter. Make enough copies for everyone in the small group. Demonstrate how to use a bookmark or ruler to cover all of the letters except the first one. Quietly say the sound that the first letter represents, repeating or holding that letter sound as you move the bookmark to the right to allow the second letter to be seen. Say that sound, holding it as you move the bookmark to the right to allow the third letter to be seen. Then, pronounce that letter sound. As you run your finger under the word, say the letter sounds again a bit more quickly. Finally, announce the word. Complete the same procedure for all of the words on the page. Repeat them, letting students join in. Let students make their own bookmarks to practice sounding out words.

Locomotive Words

Locate a small, wooden train set whose cars attach with magnets. Write each letter of a three-letter word on three self-stick notes, and attach the self-stick notes to the tops of three of the train cars. Demonstrate how to say the sound on the first train car, then hook the second train car to the first and say the second sound. Repeat with the third train car. The process of moving the train cars and linking them together helps kinesthetic learners understand the process of blending letters together to make words.

Word Families

Each week, highlight one word family, such as the -at family. Write -at on several index cards and display them in a pocket chart. Create a set of consonant cards by writing several lowercase consonants on index cards. Have small groups of students match the consonant cards to the word family by putting the consonant cards in front of the ending -at and saying the word. For example, a student might choose the letter *r*, put it in front of the -at ending, and say, "I made *rat.*"

Tap it Out

Use this activity to help students learn to blend (and segment) the sounds in words. Write a three-letter word, such as *jet*, on the board. Demonstrate how to tap your index finger and thumb together as you pronounce the first sound, /j/; tap your middle finger and thumb together as you pronounce the vowel sound, /e/; and tap your thumb and ring finger together as you pronounce the final sound, /t/. Finally, tap all of the fingers to your thumb as you pronounce the word *jet*.

Extension - Alternately, let students "tap out" the word using their arms. Each student should tap near his wrist as he pronounces the first sound, tap near his elbow for the middle sound, and finish the word by tapping the final sound near his shoulder. Students should pronounce the whole word as they sweep their hands up their arms slowly at first, then more quickly. (Extend the tapping to head, then opposite shoulder, elbow, and wrist for words with more phonemes.)

Teaching Tip

After a student has learned the short-vowel sounds, all consonants, and can read many simple three-letter words, introduce consonant blends and digraphs. The activities on the following pages will help introduce students to blends and digraphs.

Adding Letters to Make New Words

After students have had several experiences with word families, introduce a new rime. Write this rime on an index card or sentence strip and display it in a pocket chart. Distribute index cards and markers and challenge a small group of students to add one or two letters at the beginning of the rime to make new words. Initially, introduce some of the more common rimes, such as -ake, -an, -ap, -at, -ate, -eat, -ell, -est, -ice, -ide, -ill, -in, -ip, -it, -ock, -op, -ore, -ot, or -ug. As students become more accomplished at this activity, introduce some less common rimes.

Extension - Rather than giving students the rime, introduce a word and ask them to change letters at the beginning of the word to create new words. While they are still working with rimes, this changes the focus slightly to emphasize a whole word. This helps young students connect the sounds to words that have meaning for them.

 ## Word Family Dice

Make several sets of "onset dice." On each blank face of one die, write a different onset that make words when matched with a particular rime. On the other blank die in the set, write the matching rime on all six sides. (Use the list below for examples of possible onsets and rimes.) Give students two matching dice. Instruct each student to roll the dice and pronounce the sound associated with the letter on the onset die. Then, have the student blend the onset with the rime to make a word. Examples of rimes and six letters that could be written on dice:

-ad – b, d, f, h, m, s
-at – b, c, h, m, r, s
-ell – b, f, s, t, w, y
-est – b, n, p, r, t, v
-it – b, f, h, l, s, w

Extension - As students become accomplished with blending a single letter onset and simple rime, use more complex onsets with blends or digraphs. Examples of these onsets and rimes are:

-ap – ch, cl, scr, sl, sn, tr
-ash– cl, fl, sm, st, thr, tr
-ing– br, cl, spr, st, sw, th
-um– ch, dr, gl, pl, str, sw
-ush– bl, br, cr, fl, pl, sl

Building Up and Tearing Down

For this activity, provide only the letter tiles needed to create the words being used. (In the example activity, the letters would be *a*, *b*, *c*, *d*, and *t*.) Ask students to put their letter tiles in a line at the top of a table or desk. Tell them to listen very carefully as you give instructions for moving the letter tiles to make different words. For example, the instruction could be:

a	Pull down the *a*.
at	Add one letter to make the word *at*.
cat	Add one letter to make the word *cat*.
bat	Change one letter to make the word *bat*.
bad	Change one letter to make the word *bad*.
ad	Remove one letter to make the word *ad*.
a	Remove one letter to make the word *a* again.

Extension – Some students benefit from the action of snapping and unsnapping letters. Do this same activity with students using plastic, interlocking cubes. Write the letters on one side of the cubes.

Blending Stories

As you tell a familiar story to a small group of students, sound out key words. For example, say, "Once upon a time there was a little g-ir-l named Goldilocks. One d-ay she was walking in the w-oo-d-s and found a lit-tle h-ou-se," and so on. Pause after each segmented word to allow students to process blending the word. Encourage students to say the word as quickly as possible.

h-ou-se

Assessment of Blending

Use the Assessment of Blending (page 177) to evaluate students' skill in this area. Consider using both words students have studied in this unit, and also new words. Write letters of some of the chosen words on index cards, or use letter manipulatives. Have students sound out the individual letter sounds, then blend the sounds together.

Assessment of Blending

Name _____ Date _____

Recorder _____

Use this assessment to document students' blending skills. Before assessment, on a separate sheet of paper, write short lists of words you wish for students to blend. Use letter cards or other manipulatives to spell the words, keeping the letters far apart and letting students manipulate them as needed. Show each student one two-phoneme word at a time. If the student can blend letters to make a word, put a check mark in the 2P column. Write any words the student cannot name. Repeat with three-phoneme and four-phoneme words. Use the results of the assessment to plan for reteaching.

Student's Name	Two-Phoneme Words	Three-Phoneme Words	Four-Phoneme Words
SN	2P	3P	AS

Segmenting

Segmenting sounds, another part of phonemic awareness, has been defined as "the ability to notice, think about, and work with the individual sounds in spoken words. Before students learn to read print, they need to become aware of how the sounds in words work" (CIERA, 2001). But before most students segment sounds within a word, they learn to segment words within a sentence and syllables within a word. These skills typically occur after students can identify rhyming words and hear alliteration among words.

Phonemic awareness means that students are proficient at phoneme manipulation, which includes blending, segmenting, deleting, adding, and substituting phonemes. To blend phonemes, students must "combine individual phonemes to form words," or "combine onsets and rimes to make syllables or combine syllables to make words" (CIERA, 2001). To segment words into phonemes, they must do the opposite, and learn to "break words into their individual phonemes . . . They are also segmenting when they break words into syllables or divide syllables into onsets and rimes" (CIERA, 2001). Learning to segment means that students are learning to isolate the sounds, also a necessary skill for phoneme substitution, addition, and deletion, which are other important types of phoneme manipulation.

However (as stated on page 7 of the CIERA document), the National Reading Panel has determined that students who receive instruction that focuses on one or two types of phoneme manipulation make greater gains in reading and spelling than do students who are taught three or more types of manipulation. One possible explanation for this is that students who are taught many different ways to manipulate phonemes may become confused about which type to apply. Another explanation is that teaching many types of manipulations does not leave enough time to teach any one type thoroughly. A third explanation is that instruction that includes several types of manipulations may result in teaching students more difficult manipulations before they develop skill in the easier ones. Therefore, it is probably best to limit instruction to segmenting and blending sounds when developing phonemic awareness in young students.

Round and Round

In a small bag, place several objects whose names have one syllable and begin with consonants. Ask a small group of students to sit in a circle. Give the bag to a student. As students pass the bag around the circle, they should take turns removing an object from the bag, saying its name, and then segmenting the initial consonant sound (or consonant cluster, if students are ready) and the rest of the word. For example, if the object is a pen, the student would say, "/p/ /en/." The students should pass the bag around the circle until all students have had a turn.

178

Clapping Names

During the morning message, ask one student to say his name slowly. Ask the class, "Did you hear David say his name? Listen again: *Da-vid.* Do you hear two parts in his name? Okay, let's all say it together and clap the parts." Continue clapping the syllables in the names of four more students. On subsequent days, use the names of other students. Continue this activity until students have clapped the names of all classmates.

Extension – When most of the students can clap their classmates' names, clap the number of syllables in a student's name and have the class predict whose name was clapped. Each number of claps can represent more than one student. Point that out to the class, emphasizing that some questions have more than one "right" answer.

Extension – After clapping all students' names, work with them to create a chart of names that have one syllable, two syllables, three syllables, and more.

Clapping the Poem

To help students understand the concept of syllables, write a short, familiar poem on a chart tablet. Ask students to recite the poem and clap as they say each syllable. After students can do this easily, ask them to recite the poem, clap the syllables, and watch as you write a tick mark above each syllable on the poem.

Extension – If students are having difficulty clapping syllables, try having students put their fingers under their chins and count the number of times their jaws drop down when they say a word. This method is a bit more concrete for kinesthetic learners.

Extension – If students are more visual, display the cards in a pocket chart and have students copy the words, dividing them by inserting a line between syllables.

Teaching Tip

Learning to distinguish the difference between segmenting words and segmenting syllables is difficult for many students. To support this learning, use different methods for tracking the different parts. For example, if students slap knees for words in a sentence, have them clap for syllables within a word. Be consistent with the method you choose.

Introducing Syllables

Use a few two-syllable words from the class word wall to introduce the concept of syllables. Write the words on sentence strips. Read one word to the class, then cut the word on the strip into syllables. Put the word in a slot in a pocket chart, leaving a small space between the two parts of the word. (Consider dividing the syllables by placing a small piece of another color of sentence strip between them.) Have students read the word together. Repeat with other words.

179

Name that Syllable

As students learn the concept of syllables, go around the classroom and have each student say his name and then clap its syllables. Then, let him write his name on the board and draw a slash to divide the syllables. Use students' last names to repeat the activity.

Meaningful Multisyllabic Words

Use the names of objects or pictures from a unit of study to count syllables in words. This gives students additional practice in learning new vocabulary words while they expand their knowledge about syllables. For example, during a study of plants, divide garden-related terms such as *seed, catalog, hoe, spade, soil, herbs, flowers, vegetables, fertilizer,* etc., into syllables.

Multisyllabic

Teach students the word *multisyllabic.* (Young students love learning "big" words.) Explain that syllables are parts of words. Be sure to break this word into syllables for practice! After learning this word, challenge students to identify new words as multisyllabic. Let students clap the syllables of new words that they learn.

Connecting Books With Syllables

Another way to introduce "meaningful" words to students is through simple, familiar texts. On chart paper, write two-syllable words from picture books. Examples of books and words include:

- from *Five Little Monkeys Jumping on the Bed* by Eileen Christelow (Clarion Books, 1989): *monkeys, mama, doctor, jumping, goodness*

- from *The Napping House* by Audrey Wood (Red Wagon Books, 2000): *napping, sleeping, cozy, granny, snoring, dreaming, dozing, snoozing, wakeful*

- from *The Very Busy Spider* by Eric Carle (Philomel, 1995): *morning, spider, silky, body, landed, didn't, very, busy, spinning, answer, bleated, meadow, finished, rooster, pesky*

When students are able to easily distinguish between one- and two-syllable words, try sharing three- to five-syllable words from familiar books. Some examples might be:

- from *Families* by Ann Morris (HarperCollins, 2000): *everyone, everywhere, family, another, together, celebrate, stepparents, grandparent, specially, wherever*

- from *Franklin Plays the Game* by Paulette Bourgeois (Scholastic, 1995): *uniforms, intended, forgetting, goalkeeper, important, everybody, untangle*

- from *A House is a House for Me* by Mary Ann Hoberman (Puffin, 1982): *mosquitoes, Eskimo, pueblo, terminal, farfetching, reflections, envelopes, tablecloths, whatever*

- from *Is a Dolphin a Fish?: Questions and Answers about Dolphins* by Melvin and Gilda Berger (Scholastic, 2002): *ancestors, familiar, undersides, energy, various, automatically, scientists, cetaceans, porpoises* (selected words)

Up and Down

Say a two-syllable word. Ask students to repeat the word; each student should raise an arm above her head for each syllable. Have students say the word again, dropping one arm as they say the first syllable and dropping the other arm as they say the second syllable. Then, ask them to repeat the word again.

What's Left?

After modeling segmenting the onset from the rime of many words, present a word to students, and ask them to respond with the rime only. For example, say, "If you take away the beginning sound from *rice*, you make _____?" Students should respond, "ice." This activity can be done with any word, but is more effective when the words mean something to students. Use names of students in the class, names of popular toys or television programs, favorite books or characters, or words from particular interest areas such as soccer, dinosaurs, etc.

Picture P-ar-t-s

Cut pictures of two- and three-phoneme words into either two or three parts. For example, cut a picture of a fish into three parts, a hoe into two parts, a leaf into three parts, etc. Ask students to move the parts of the picture together as they say the sounds. When all of the parts are together, ask them to say the whole word.

> **Teaching Tip**
> After students understand the concept of syllables, prevent them from getting confused as they learn to segment the sounds within syllables (onsets and rimes, and individual phonemes) by using only monosyllabic words at first.

 The Button Game

Complete this activity as a small-group or whole-group activity. Copy the Phoneme-Counting Rectangles (page 183) for each student. (Use the three-space rectangle for three-phoneme words and the four-space rectangle for words with four phonemes.) Give one rectangle and three buttons to each student. Say a three-letter/three phoneme word, such as *bat*, very slowly. Have students push a button onto a rectangle to represent each sound they hear—in this case, /b/ /a/ /t/. Have students check with each other to confirm how many buttons they have in their boxes. As students become more experienced, work with longer words. (To work with words that are five-phonemes and larger, create additional phoneme-counting rectangles.)

Simon Says

Vary the traditional "Simon Says" game to focus on segmenting words into parts. Say a one-syllable command word, such as *talk*, and break the word into its onset and rime. For example, pronounce *talk* as "/t/ /alk/." Challenge students to repeat the word by blending it together, and perform the action, but only if you said "Simon says." When you do not say "Simon Says," the students should not do anything. For example, say, "Simon says /j/ /ump/." Students should say "jump" and start to jump. Say, "Simon says /st/ /op/," and students should say, "Stop," and stop jumping. Continue with other one-syllable command words, like *walk, jog, bend, hop, flap, sit, clap, dance, wink, wave,* etc.

Write the Sound

Distribute a write-on/wipe-away board and marker to each student, or have students use pencils and paper. Carefully pronounce letter sounds one at a time and ask students to write the letter that is associated with the sound you say. Then, ask students to write their names on their papers or boards. Maintain your own list as you say the sounds. Then, collect students' lists and use them to assess this skill.

Teaching Tip

Write-on/wipe-away boards can be expensive. Instead, purchase shower board at a local building supply store. This typically comes in large sheets. Store personnel are usually willing to cut the sheets into smaller pieces.

Teaching Tip

Store all write-on/wipe-away markers inside inexpensive socks, one marker per sock. You can ask families to donate worn-out, but clean, socks. Instruct each student to put the sock over the hand she does not use to write, and use the sock as an eraser. Storing the marker inside the sock makes passing out materials more time-efficient.

182

Phoneme-Counting Rectangles

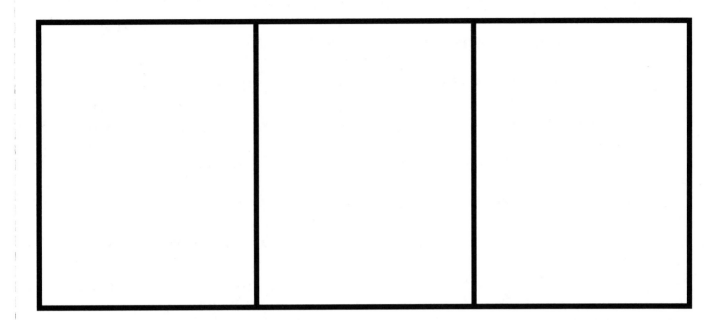

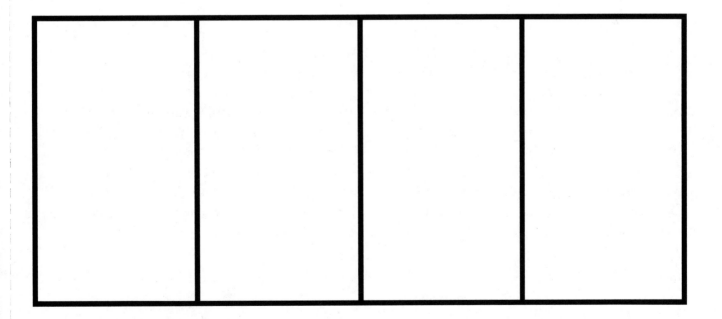

● ● Cookie Sheet Sounds

Line up a set of magnetic letters at the top of a cookie sheet. Include these letters: *d, g, l, o, r, c, a, t*. Create five additional cookie sheets with identical letter sets. Sit with students in a circle on the floor. Ask them to listen carefully as you say words very slowly. Tell them that they are to spell the words you say. Give students several seconds to hear each sound in the word, scan the letters to locate the letter associated with the sound you say, and pull that letter down to the center of the cookie sheet. Initially, choose short, simple words such as *dog, cat, rat,* etc. Then, move to more complex words such as *card, glad,* etc.

● ● Spell the Object

Begin teaching students to isolate medial sounds. Collect several items with short names that have short or long vowel sounds in the middle of them. Suggested objects are: *bat, fan, beads, flag, pan, cap, bib, kite, dice, egg, bread, can, vase, peas, peach,* etc. Show items one at a time and ask students to name the object, repeat the word very slowly, and then write the letter sounds they hear. Support students as they pronounce each word by emphasizing the medial vowel sound.

Teaching Tip

When you first begin the Cookie Sheet Sounds activity (left), ask students to locate only the initial sound in the word. After they are comfortable with that skill, extend the lesson to require the students to spell the whole word, gradually increasing the difficulty of the words. Finally, ask students to identify only the final sound in the word.

Beginning, Middle, or End?

Give each student a game marker. (Game markers can be two-color counters, checkers, buttons, etc.). Also give each student an index card or copy the box portion of the Phoneme-Counting Rectangles reproducible (page 183) for each student. Have each student draw two lines in a straight row on the index card to divide it into three sections. Say one letter sound and write the letter that makes that sound on the board. Then, present a series of words that contain that sound at the beginning, in the middle, or at the end. Students should indicate where the sound is in each word by placing their markers in the appropriate square. For example, for /m/, say the words *March, man, watermelon, hamburger, them, trim*. Observe where students place their markers, noting which students place them in the correct positions.

● ● Shoot the Arrow

Assign students to small groups. Make copies of the Shoot the Arrow game board (page 186) on several pieces of card stock. Create one board for each group. Instruct the students in each group to place two or three markers on the top line of their game boards. Say a word with two or three phonemes. As you say each sound, place the marker that represents the first phoneme over the dot. Place the other markers from left to right, using the arrow as a guide. After students move their markers, they should repeat the word, sweeping their hand under the markers as they slowly say the word.

Extension – To familiarize students with new words, play this game using short sentences. Ask each student to slide a marker to the arrow each time she hears a predetermined word pronounced in a sentence.

B verses D Words

Enlarge, color, and cut out the B verses D Words patterns (page 187). Glue them to the inside of a file folder, leaving ample writing space underneath. Draw a writing line on the folder under each picture. Copy and cut out the directions (page 187). Glue the directions to the front of the folder and glue the answer key to the back. Laminate the folder. Have each student use a write-on/wipe-away pen to write the name of each object on the line drawn under its picture, then check her answers. Since standard or phonemic spellings are acceptable, consider adding sound spellings that your students will recognize to the answer key.

Changing Names

Call students' names to take attendance, but change their names. Explain to students what you are doing and ask them to listen very carefully for their changed names. Delete the first sound of all names. For example, Mary becomes Ary, Jorge becomes Orge, and Chen becomes En.

Extension - Change students' names by substituting all of the first initial sounds with the same sound. For example, Mary becomes Dary, Jorge becomes Dorge, Chen becomes Den, and so on.

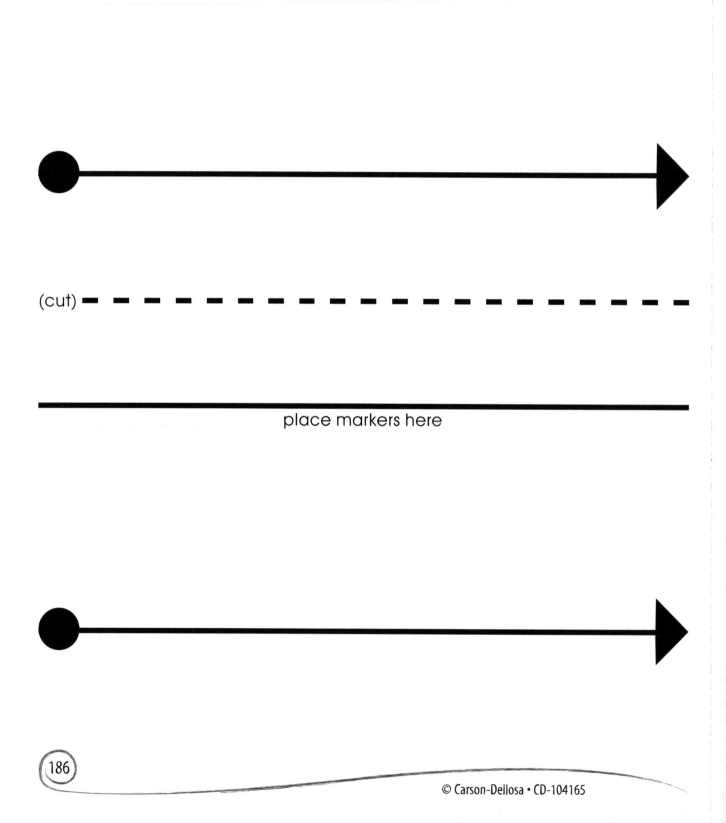

place markers here

(cut)

place markers here

Directions: Say each word very slowly. On the line under each picture, write all of the letters you hear in each word. Look at the answer key to check your work.

Answer Key: ball, boot, bone, book, bow, box, bus, dart, deer, dice, desk, dog, doll, domino

Segmenting Poems

Use this poetry activity to challenge students' segmenting skills. In the area where you will complete this activity, display an alphabet chart, such as the one from page 19. (Enlarge this page, if necessary.) Write a simple rhyming verse on the board, leaving out the second rhyming word. For example, write: *Jack Sprat could eat no _____ .* First, let students identify the rhyming word (Sprat). Then, let students take turns substituting the first letter of that word with a letter of the alphabet. When first doing this activity, have students replace letters in alphabetical order. Write all of the new "words" on the board. Within this list, identify all real words they created, such as *bat, cat, hat,* etc. Then, ask if each word makes sense. When students decide that the word should be *fat,* write the entire phrase on the board. Note: When choosing rhymes for this activity, complete the alphabet substitution yourself first, to make sure that all "created" words are appropriate for the classroom. If you come across inappropriate words that can be made, simply make a list of letters that students should use.

Move That Letter

Sit with a small group and use a write-on/wipe-away marker to write a word on the board that can be made into a smaller word when one letter is taken away. For example, if you write the word *cat,* the letter *c* can be removed to make the word *at.* After writing the word, let students take turns telling you which letter to take away. As they guess letters, erase them one at a time and pronounce the new word, then write the new word under the original. If students are correct, write a new word on the board. If more than one option is correct, as in the word *pants,* list all of the new words (*pans, ants, pant, pan, pat*). Be sure to pronounce all of the new words and let students identify the sounds as well as the letters that have been removed. As students become better at this activity, use longer words, or let students remove more than one letter. Some possible words are listed below. A helpful way to think of new words for this activity is to do this backward; that is, to build larger words from smaller ones. Start with a small word like *am* and build larger ones from it (*am, ham, harm, charm*). Possible words to use: *fist (fit, it), smiles (smile, miles, mile), steal (seal, teal, tea), clean (lean, clan, can), swarms (warms, warm, arm),* and *beast (best, bet, east, eat).*

Substitute Riddles

Use the minute or two before lunch to ask children riddles based on phoneme substitutions:

• What rhymes with *call* and is used to play soccer?
• What do men wear around their necks that rhymes with *fly*?
• What rhymes with *Dan* and is used to fry eggs?

"Row, Row, Row Your Boat" Substitution

Sing the first verse of "Row, Row, Row Your Boat" in the traditional way. For subsequent verses, change initial sounds of key words within a verse to the same sound. For example, for /b/, sing:

Bow, bow, bow your boat,
Bently bown the beam.
Berrily, berrily, berrily, berrily,
Bife is but a beam.

For /m/, sing:
Mow, mow, mow your moat,
Mently mown the meam.
Merrily, merrily, merrily, merrily,
Mife is mut a meam.

Verses can also be created for blends or digraphs:

For /bl/, sing:
Blow, blow, blow your bloat,
Blently blown the bleam.
Blerrily, blerrily, blerrily, blerrily,
Blife is blut a bleam.

For /sh/, sing:
Show, show, show your shoat,
Shently shown the sheam.
Sherrily, sherrily, sherrily, sherrily,
Shife is shut a sheam.

S.S. Shoat

Assessment of Segmenting

Use the form on page 190 to document students' capabilities in segmenting.

Assessment of Segmenting

Use this form to document students' segmenting abilities. When you observe students doing the following skills, make a note in the column of the day's date and what the child said or did to prove competence in these skills: Slaps Words in a Sentence, Claps Syllables in a Word, Segments Three-Phoneme Words, and Segments Four-Phoneme Words.

Student's Name	Date	Slaps Words in a Sentence	Claps Syllables in a Word	Segments Three-Phoneme Words	Segments Four-Phoneme Words
SN	D	SW	CS	3P	4P

Sight Words

Students need a strong sight word vocabulary to become competent, successful readers. Sight words are common words that students first see in beginning readers' stories. Many of the first 50 words that experts designate as beginning sight words are two- and three-letter words. Words like *is, am, it, up, a,* and *if* need to be automatically recognized by beginning readers.

For the most part, sight words must be memorized. However, connecting sight words to something that is meaningful to students helps with the process. If that is possible, it helps students learn the sight words more quickly. For example, if the class is familiar with Eric Carle's work, they can connect the word *the* to his books, such as *The Very Hungry Caterpillar, The Very Busy Spider, The Very Quiet Cricket,* and so on.

Using Sight Word Lists

To support students as they develop a vocabulary of sight words, select a few new words to teach each week. Be sure the words that you select look as unlike as possible so they are easier for students to remember. Write each word on a 3" x 5" index card. Show one word to a small group of students, and say: "This is the word *if.*" Then, ask the group, "What letter is at the beginning of this word?" If appropriate, ask, "Does this word have a smaller word inside of it?" Next, try to point out something characteristic about the word, such as, "This word begins with the same letter as your name," or "This word only has three letters, just like the word *cat* you learned yesterday." Then, say, "I will say each letter in the word aloud, and you should write it in the sand." (Use any appropriate kinesthetic writing tools, like shaving cream on a cookie sheet, chalk on the sidewalk, magnetic letters, cereal letters, etc.) Then, have students spell the word aloud.

Teaching Tip

Before teaching sight words, let each student make a sight word book by stapling writing paper between card stock covers. Let students decorate their word books with letter stamps. Each time you teach a new group of sight words, make sure students record the words in their word books.

Creating and Using Word Walls

In a prominent place in the classroom, create a word wall where there is a designated space for words that begin with each letter of the alphabet. Introduce five new sight words to the class each Monday, then on the other mornings lead students in an activity to reinforce those words. Use the following activities (pages 192–193) with the word wall.

Extension – Post a simple picture or drawing by you or a student next to the nouns or verbs that can be illustrated. For example, beside *boy* draw a simple stick figure of a boy or by *run* draw a simple sketch of a person with knees and arms bent in a running pose. Discuss with students why some of the words cannot have pictures that represent them.

A
apple
an
at

B
be
boy

C
can
car

N
no
nose

O
octopus

P
pencil
put

Portable Word Walls

Create portable word walls that students can use outside, in the library, at home, etc. Have students create portable word walls by dividing each of the four "pages" of a file folder (the front, two inside pages, and back) into six smaller sections. Give each letter its own section in the portable word wall, putting x, y, and z in the same section. Have students recreate the class word wall on their folders.

The Rhythm of Words

Read a new sight word while making it a rhythmic experience. Spell the word while clapping one clap per letter (or snapping fingers, stomping feet, tapping shoulders, jumping in the air, etc.), and then read the word again. Have students repeat the motions and spelling with you.

Guess My Word

Have students write numerals 1 through 5 down the left side of a piece of paper. Silently choose a word from the word wall. Give clues for the word that you are thinking about, starting with more difficult clues and ending with easy clues. Have students write down their guesses after hearing each clue. For example, if the word is *they*, say:

1. It is a word on the word wall.
2. It has one syllable.
3. It starts with a digraph.
4. It ends with the long /a/ sound, but it is not spelled with an *a*.
5. It means more than one person.

Last Letter First

After the word wall has multiple words under most of the letters, teach small groups of students to play "Last Letter First." Have a student read a word from the word wall. The student to his right should identify the last letter in the word and then find and read a word from the word wall that begins with that letter. The next student should identify the last letter in that word, etc.

Tic-Tac-Toe

Draw a tic-tac-toe grid on the board. Copy the word cards (pages 195–204) onto card stock and cut them apart. (The words are listed alphabetically, not in order of difficulty. Use the blank cards to add words, if desired.) Assign half of the class to the X team and the other half to the O team. Write words in the tic-tac-toe spaces. Take turns having a member of the X team come up to the board and select a word to read. If she is correct, she may put an X over the space. If she is incorrect, allow the O team to send a player to the board to try to read the same word. Play several games using different sight words, and allow both teams an equal number of chances to go first.

Extension – Give everyone a blank copy of the tic-tac-toe grid (page 194), and put the list of words on the board. Have them place the words where they want on their board. As you call out the words, you say if it is an X word or an O word. The first student with three Xs or three Os in a row is the winner.

> ### Teaching Tip
> Adapt this activity to your sight words program by using words as you introduce them. Add more words over time using the additional words and the blank card template (page 204).

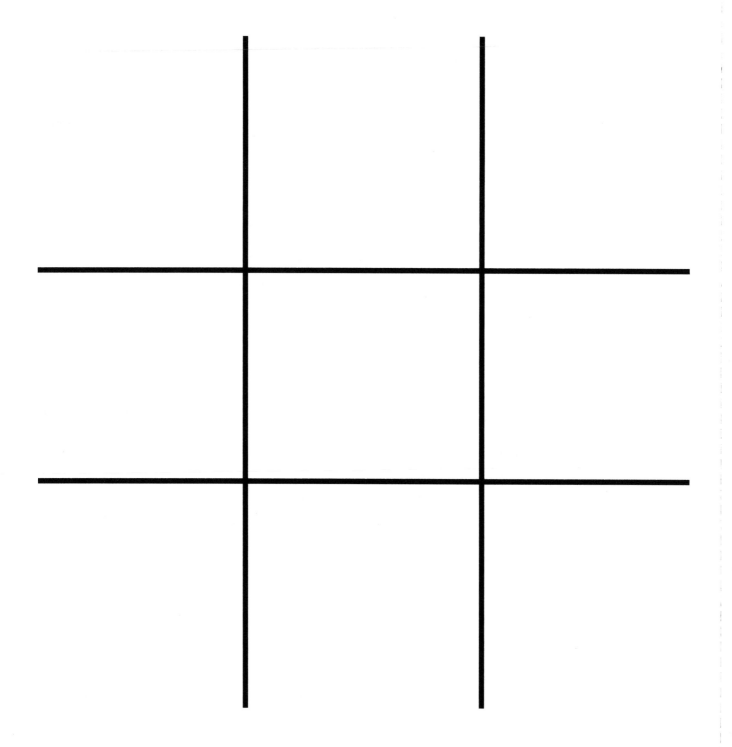

a	about	after
again	all	am
and	any	are
ask	at	ate
away	be	because

been	before	big
black	blue	both
boy	bring	brown
but	by	came
can	come	could

did	do	does
down	eat	every
favorite	find	first
for	friend	get
girl	go	good

green	has	have
he	here	how
I	into	is
it	jump	knew
know	let	like

little	made	make
many	may	me
more	much	must
my	myself	new
no	now	of

off	on	once
one	open	orange
other	our	out
own	play	please
pretty	pull	purple

put	ran	read
red	ride	right
said	saw	say
see	she	so
sometimes	soon	tell

thank	that	the
them	there	these
they	think	this
to	today	together
too	under	up

us	use	very
want	was	we
well	went	what
when	where	which
white	who	why

will	with	yellow
yes	you	your

Go Fishing for Words

Choose eight words from the list of sight word cards (pages 195–204). Write each word on a set of four index cards to create 32 total cards. Give the deck to a group of three students. Demonstrate how to play Go Fish using these sight word cards. Have a student deal five cards to each player. Then, have the player to the left of the dealer ask another player for one of the word cards she has. Explain that students should try to get sets of all four words. When a student has four identical words, she should place them in front of her in a stack. The student with the most stacks wins the game.

Sight Word Concentration

Use two cards from each of the four-card sets from the Go Fishing for Words activity (above) to create a deck to use for concentration. Place the cards facedown on the table in a grid design. Have students take turns turning over two cards at a time. If the cards do not match, the student should turn the cards facedown. If the cards match and the student can read the word, the student should keep the cards. It is then the next student's turn. The student with the most matches is the winner.

BANG!

This simple game encourages students to practice reading sight words. Write each sight word that has been introduced to the class on an index card. Also write the word *Bang!* on several cards. Put the cards in a large can or similar container. Have the first student close his eyes, pick a card, and read it aloud. If he picks a sight word card and reads it correctly, he should keep the card, and it is the next student's turn. If he picks a card with the word *bang*, he should say, "Bang!" loudly and return all of his cards to the container. Designate a time period for the game. The student with the most cards at the end of the time period wins the game.

Compound Break-Apart

Use compound words to teach the shorter words within them. Say a compound word such as *butterfly*. Then, say the word again, leaving off the second part: "butter_____." Ask for a volunteer to supply the missing part. Write the short word *fly* on the board. Play again, asking students to supply the first part as you say the last part.

> ### Teaching Tip
> If a student needs to practice writing sight words to reinforce his memory, ask him to write the sight word cards for Go Fishing for Words (left) and other word card activities. This provides necessary practice and lets the student feel he is doing something important for the class.

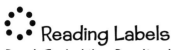

Reading Labels

Read *Carlo Likes Reading* by Jessica Spanyol (Candlewick, 2001) to the class. In this book, Carlo's environment, from the rooms in his house to his yard, to a bakery shop and a vegetable market, are all labeled. Modeling Carlo's environment, work with students to post labels on objects in the classroom. Because students can become overwhelmed if too many classroom labels are posted at one time, post one label per day. Students will pay more attention to the labels when they are involved in the labeling process (deciding what to label, posting the labels themselves, chorally "reading" the labels as a class, or working in pairs and "reading" labels to each other). To draw students' attention back to these labels, rename all previously labeled objects each time you add a new label. Make sure, however, to pay appropriate attention to the new label.

Sentence Steps

Have students stand in a line in an open space. As you say a simple sentence, ask students to take a step forward for each word that you say. Then, ask how many words were in the sentence by having them recall how many steps they took. For example, if you said "The red ball bounced," students would take four steps, then repeat the sentence. It is sometimes helpful for the students to count using their fingers as you say the sentence. Vary the game by asking students to walk backward, sideways, take giant steps, take baby steps, etc.

Erase Relay

Assign students to two teams. Have the teams stand in a line so that the first student in line faces the chalkboard. On the board, create two columns of words that are approximately equal in difficulty level. Write as many words on the board as there are students in the relay. At the signal, the first student in each line should walk to the board, point to the first word in his team's column of words, and pronounce that word. If he pronounces it correctly, he should erase that word and go to the back of the line. The team that erases all of the words first is the winner.

Spelling Sight Words

Use a blank game board, or copy one from this book (pages 96–97). Give it to a small group along with a die and game pieces. Join the group to play this spelling game. Have students roll the die to see who goes first. Then, have the winner roll the die again. Before she moves, say a sight word for her to spell. If she spells the word correctly, she may move the number of spaces on the die. If she spells it incorrectly, show the word to the student for a few seconds, then hide it. Allow her to spell the word again. If the student spells the word correctly, she should move the number indicated on the die, minus one. (If the student rolled a one, she does not move her game piece.) If she spells it incorrectly, she does not move her game piece. While the next student is rolling, the previous student should write the word on a piece of paper if she could not spell it. At the end of the game, students will have a list of words that they need to learn how to spell.

Finger Play: Bear Hunt

Incorporate this familiar chant and its accompanying actions with a sight word study. Write the names of each action or preposition describing an action (see, go, over, etc.) on cards and ask students to arrange them in the order of the story.

Let's go on a bear hunt. (Slap hands on a table to make a walking sound.)

I see a wheat field. Can't go over it. Let's go through it. (Brush hands together.)

I see a bridge. Can't go around it. Let's go over it. (Slap hands together.)

I see a lake. Can't go over it, can't go under it, let's swim across it. (Arms swimming.)

I see a tree. Can't go over it, can't go under it, let's go up it. (Climb with arms.)

I don't see any bears. (Look around.) Let's go down. (Pretend to walk downhill.)

I see a swamp. Can't go over it, can't go under it, let's go through it. (Pull hands up and down slowly.)

I see a cave. Can't go over it, can't go under it, let's go in. (Slowly slap knees.)

I see two eyes. I see two ears.

I see a nose. I see a mouth.

Yikes! It's a bear!!!

Let's get out of here! (Reverse movements very quickly.)

Teaching Tip

Search discount stores and tag sales for bargains on commercially produced games. It is a good idea to make some game boards with fewer spaces and some with more. Then you can choose which board to play depending on the amount of time available. After purchase, adapt the game boards to support learning and practicing literacy skills. Use small, round (tag sale) stickers and a permanent marker to change game boards.

References

Armbruster, Bonnie, B., F. Lehr, and J. Osborn. Center for the Improvement of Early Reading Achievement (CIERA). 2001. *Put Reading First: The Research Building Blocks for Teaching Children to Read.* Ann Arbor, MI

Johnston, F. R. 1999. The timing and teaching of word families. *The Reading Teacher* 53:64-75.

Morrow, L. M. and D. H. Tracey. 1997. Strategies used for phonics instruction in early childhood classrooms. *The Reading Teacher* 50:644–651.

Moustafa, M. and Maldonado-Colon, E. 1999. Whole-to-parts phonics instruction: Building on what children know to help them know more. *The Reading Teacher,* 52:448–458.

Pinnell, G. S. and I. C. Fountas. 1998. *Word Matters: Teaching Phonics and Spelling in the Reading/ Writing Classroom.* Portsmouth, NH: Heinemann.

Neuman, S. B. C. Copple, and S. Bredekamp. 2000. *Learning to Read and Write: Developmentally Appropriate Practices for Young Children.* Washington, DC: National Association for the Education of Young Children.

Opitz, M. 2000. *Rhymes and Reasons: Literature and Language Play for Phonological Awareness.* Portsmouth, NH: Heinemann.

Shaywitz, S. 2003. *Overcoming Dyslexia: A New and Complete Science-Based Program for Reading Problems at Any Level.* New York: Knopf.

Smith, J. A. 2000. Singing and songwriting support early literacy instruction. *The Reading Teacher,* 53:646–649.

Snow, C. E., M. S. Burns, and P. Griffin, eds. 1998. *Preventing Reading Difficulties in Young Children.* Washington, DC: National Academies Press.

Wasik, B. L. 2001. Phonemic awareness and young children. *Childhood Education:* 77(3), 128-133.